P9-APF-620

Building
Bridges

Building Bridges

An Egypt-U.S. Free Trade Agreement

AHMED GALAL
ROBERT Z. LAWRENCE
Editors

THE EGYPTIAN CENTER FOR ECONOMIC STUDIES
Cairo

JOHN F. KENNEDY SCHOOL OF GOVERNMENT
Cambridge, Massachusetts

BROOKINGS INSTITUTION PRESS / *Washington, D.C.*

Copyright © 1998 by
THE EGYPTIAN CENTER FOR ECONOMIC STUDIES
JOHN F. KENNEDY SCHOOL OF GOVERNMENT

Building Bridges: An Egypt-U.S. Free Trade Agreement
may be ordered from:

Brookings Institution Press
1775 Massachusetts Avenue, N.W.
Washington, D.C. 20036
Telephone: 1-800/275-1447 or 202/797-6258
Fax: 202/797-6004
Internet: www.brook.edu

Library of Congress Cataloging-in-Publication data
Building bridges : An Egypt-U.S. free trade agreement / Ahmed Galal
and Robert Z. Lawrence, editors.
    p.   cm.
Includes bibliographical references.
ISBN 0-8157-3030-6 (cloth : alk. paper)
    1. United States—Foreign economic relations—Egypt. 2. Egypt—
Foreign economic relations—United States. 3. United States—
Commercial treaties. 4. Egypt—Commercial treaties. 5. Free trade—
United States. 6. Free trade—Egypt. I. Galal, Ahmed, 1948–
II. Lawrence, Robert Z., 1949–

HF1456.5.E3 E34   1998   98-25421
382'.0973062—ddc21   CIP

9 8 7 6 5 4 3 2 1

The paper used in this publication meets the minimum requirements of the
American National Standard for Information Sciences—Permanence of
Paper for Printed Library Materials, ANSI Z39.48-1984

Typeset in Palatino

Composition by Cynthia Stock
Silver Spring, Maryland

Printed by R. R. Donnelley and Sons
Harrisonburg, Virginia

Preface

IS A FREE TRADE agreement between Egypt and the United States an idea whose time has come? The very question will strike many readers as novel. While no one doubts the importance of the strategic relationship between Egypt and the United States, few focus on the relationship's economic dimensions. Yet economic reform in Egypt and the shift in U.S. trade policy toward an increased emphasis on regional free trade agreements lead quite naturally to this question. In this study, the authors explore the conditions under which such an agreement is likely to be most beneficial to both nations and evaluate the likely impact on both economies.

This project was initiated by the Egyptian Center for Economic Studies (ECES) in response to a request from the Presidential Council (an advisory body of Egyptian and American business executives and initiated by President Hosni Mubarak and Vice President Al Gore). The effort was later supported by Harvard University's John F. Kennedy School of Government, under the directorship of Leonard Hausman, which provided financial support to one of the authors and organized a seminar at the Brookings Institution in Washington. ECES subsequently organized a conference in Cairo to present the papers to a wider audience.

From inception to completion, the project benefited from the support, encouragement, and insights of several individuals. We are grateful to all of them. We are especially grateful to the contributing authors and discussants of the papers at the Brookings workshop and the Cairo conference. We are also grateful to the Egyptian ministers of trade (Ahmed El-Goweili) and economy

v

(Youssef Boutros Ghali) for their input at the Cairo conference and support throughout the project. Taher Helmy and Galal El Zorba (chairman and vice chairman of the board of directors of ECES) were the impetus for the project and provided support thereafter. For outstanding organization, we thank Hisham Fahmy (deputy director of ECES) and his crew, who helped to organize the Cairo conference, and Shula Gilad of the Kennedy School of Government and Ahkram Awad, who organized the Brookings seminar. Amal Refaat (ECES) provided exceptional research assistance. Last, but not least, we would like to thank Robert Faherty (director, Brookings Institution Press) for his assistance in publishing this book and Vicky Macintyre for careful editing of the manuscript, as well as Carlotta Ribar for proofreading and Susan Fels for indexing the pages.

Contents

Building
Bridges

CHAPTER ONE

Overview

Ahmed Galal and Robert Z. Lawrence

IN APRIL 1997 President Hosni Mubarak and Vice President Albert Gore agreed to explore the possibility of creating a free trade agreement (FTA) between Egypt and the United States. Although viewed with surprise in some quarters, this initiative reflects an important development in the policies of both nations. For Egypt, it signals a commitment to liberalize the economy further and integrate into the world economy. For the United States, it signals a willingness to promote the economic dimension of the U.S.-Egyptian relationship, which has hitherto primarily emphasized strategic and political considerations. It also represents a further step toward broadening the web of preferential arrangements between the United States and its trading partners.

That both sides are prepared to consider an FTA is by itself a significant development. The specifics of the agreement now need to be spelled out, studied, and negotiated, especially to appease those who are skeptical about both its desirability and feasibility. Critics in both countries oppose trade liberalization and view globalization as a trend to be resisted rather than promoted. Others support free trade in principle, but only if it is achieved through multilateral rather than preferential trade agreements.[1] Still others believe an FTA may be good in principle but impractical, in part because major steps still need to be taken to open up the Egyptian economy more fully. Also, the U.S. administration is having difficulty obtaining so-called fast-track authority from the Congress to negotiate trade agreements of high priority for the

1

United States, such as the extension of the North American Free Trade Agreement (NAFTA) to Chile (a country whose liberalization has proceeded much further than that of Egypt), free trade in the Americas and in the Asia Pacific (APEC), and additional liberalization at the World Trade Organization (WTO).

Nonetheless, as explained more fully in the following chapters, the case for considering an FTA between Egypt and the United States rests on solid economic and political grounds. The economic case is based on compelling evidence that freer trade and investment generally enhance welfare and growth; the recognition that an FTA between Egypt and the United States could help promote Egyptian economic reform and growth; and the economic benefits to the United States. There is also evidence that preferential trade agreements, if properly crafted, can act as a complement rather than an obstacle to complete liberalization. As the saying goes, the devil lies in the details. The political case rests on the crucial role Egypt plays for the United States in helping to achieve peace and maintain a stable supply of oil in the Middle East, as indicated by the magnitude of U.S. aid to Egypt ($2.3 billion a year).

Although the current political tide in the United States does not favor concluding trade agreements, that is not a reason to stop considering them. On the contrary, an understanding of the potential benefits of such agreements can help turn the current tide. Furthermore, although Egypt has not completed its reform process, important measures in recent years have prepared it to take advantage of an FTA with its major trading partners.[2] If anything, the need to stimulate further reform is an argument in favor of an FTA rather than a reason for delay.

Other developments make the case for an agreement even more compelling for both countries. To begin with, Egypt has already signed an FTA with the Arab countries and has taken major steps toward signing an FTA with the European Union. As these agreements are implemented and their competitors begin to enjoy duty-free access to Egypt, American exporters will be increasingly at a disadvantage in the Egyptian market. According to a recent study, major trading partners with Egypt, such as the United

States, are likely to respond by demanding that Egypt open its market to them.[3] Similarly, Egyptian producers are keen on securing access to American markets in a way that will match the duty-free access accorded Israel (because of the U.S.-Israel FTA), Canada and Mexico (through NAFTA), and perhaps other Latin American and Asian producers. Accordingly, pressure will mount on both sides in favor of an FTA.

A second issue relates to aid, which indicates Egypt's strategic importance to U.S. interests, but this aid is under budgetary pressures in the United States. As a result of these pressures, together with Israel's strong economic performance, plans are already under way to gradually eliminate economic assistance to Israel. Although the case for U.S. economic assistance to Egypt is much stronger, in view of the lower level of development there, any attempt to reduce it will lead the United States to provide Egypt with alternative benefits.

The discussion in this book is therefore timely and relevant for both Egyptian and U.S. policymakers, as well as for a broader group of policymakers, as it addresses such questions as: What form should an FTA agreement take? In particular, should it concentrate primarily on border barriers, or should it cover other aspects of deeper economic integration, such as investment and services? What are the likely implications of an Egypt-U.S. FTA for Egypt? What are the implications for the United States? How will such an agreement affect the rest of the region?

The book explores these questions from three perspectives: the impact on the Egyptian economy, the implications for the U.S. economy, and the implications for both countries, especially Egypt, given Egypt's other regional free trade agreements. The rest of this chapter provides an overview of the current economic relationship between Egypt and the United States and the major conclusions of the book.

Egypt-U.S. Economic Relationship

Although the economic relationship between Egypt and the United States is asymmetric, since Egypt is a much smaller economy, it is important to both countries. It encompasses trade in goods and services, capital inflows, and a significant transfer of aid to Egypt. The striking feature of the trade relationship is its concentration in a few activities. Egypt's exports to the United States are limited mainly to textiles and oil, while U.S. exports are concentrated in agricultural products and arms; U.S. investment in Egypt is virtually confined to the oil sector. Aid flows dominate the activities in trade and investment, and, overall, the United States runs a substantial trade surplus.

Trade

After the European Union (collectively), the United States is Egypt's second major trading partner in imports, supplying almost one-fifth of its imports (figure 1-1). By contrast, Egypt's exports to the United States are more modest, amounting to less than $1 billion a year. Although these represent about 10 percent of Egypt's total exports, they constitute less than a tenth of a percent of all U.S. imports, placing Egypt far down in the ranks of U.S. suppliers. Despite the rise in exports to the United States since 1989, the trade deficit between the two countries has increased.

Figure 1-1. *Egypt's Trade Pattern, 1995*
Share in total imports/exports (percent)

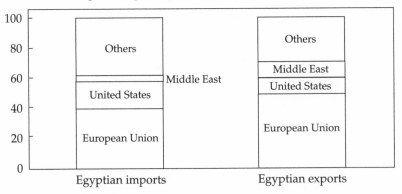

Source: International Monetary Fund (1996).

Figure 1-2. *Egypt-U.S. Trade Balance, 1989–95*

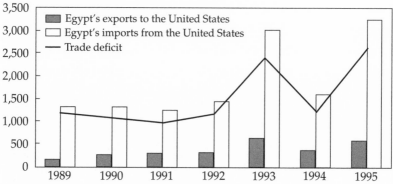

Source: International Monetary Fund (1996).

The size of the deficit—it reached $2.6 billion in 1995—is insignificant for an economy as large as the United States, but it accounts for half of Egypt's total exports in the same year (figure 1-2).

As already mentioned, trade between the two countries is highly concentrated. In 1996 Egypt's imports of wheat and maize from the United States accounted for 34.5 percent of its total imports, while arms and ammunition accounted for 13 percent. The remaining principal imports are aircraft, plant and equipment for civil engineering and contractors, paper and paperboard, and telecommunications equipment, which account for 16 percent of the total. Since some of these items are tied to U.S. aid, a decline in aid will diminish U.S. exports to Egypt. As figure 1-3 shows, Egypt's main exports to the United States in 1996 included ready-made garments (38 percent of total exports), other textile fabrics and accessories (12 percent), and mineral fuel oil and its distilled products (34 percent).

Foreign Direct Investment

U.S. investment in Egypt as of the end of 1995 was $1.41 billion. This level is relatively modest compared with U.S. foreign

Figure 1-3. *Composition of Egyptian Exports and Imports to the United States, 1996*

Share in total imports/exports (percent)

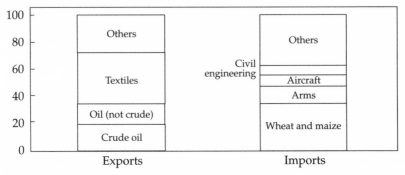

Source: Calculated from U.S. Department of Commerce data.

direct investment (FDI) in Latin America and East Asia. Brazil, for example, received as much as $23.6 billion in U.S. FDI by 1994, and Mexico received $14 billion (figure 1-4).

Although Egypt received almost as much U.S. FDI as Turkey (with a stock of U.S. FDI of $1.17 billion by 1995) and Israel ($1.57 billion by 1995), the bulk of it (76 percent) went to Egypt's oil sector and only 7.7 percent to manufacturing. In contrast, the manufacturing sector in Israel and Turkey received 70 percent and 61 percent, respectively, of total U.S. FDI (figure 1-5).

The low level of U.S. FDI in Egypt and its concentration in the oil sector may be attributed to the limited attraction of the Egyptian economy compared with alternative investment opportunities in the Far East and the emerging economies in Latin America. This situation is changing, however (see chapter 3). The new economic landscape in Egypt in the 1990s has created a more attractive market for FDI than in the past.

Aid

U.S. aid to Egypt has been the most significant component of the economic relationship between the two countries since 1979. Egypt has consistently received some $2.3 billion a year, making

Figure 1-4. *U.S. Foreign Direct Investment (FDI) in Egypt and Selected Countries, 1995*

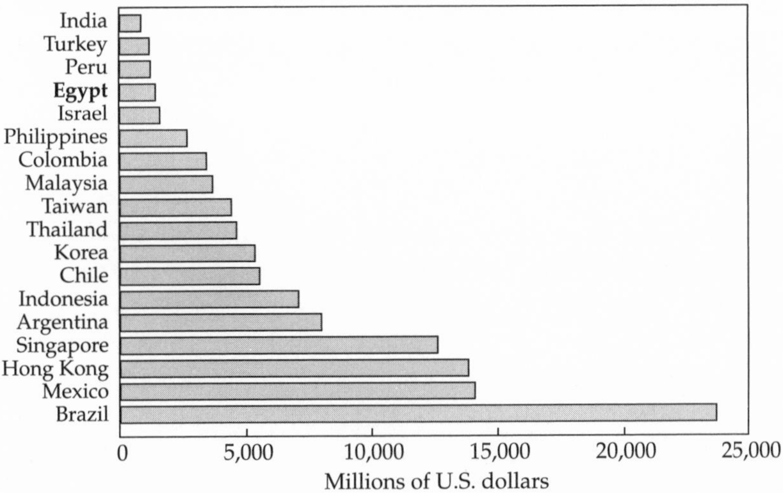

India
Turkey
Peru
Egypt
Israel
Philippines
Colombia
Malaysia
Taiwan
Thailand
Korea
Chile
Indonesia
Argentina
Singapore
Hong Kong
Mexico
Brazil
0
5,000
10,000
15,000
20,000
25,000
Millions of U.S. dollars

Source: U.S. Department of State, Country Reports on Economic Policy and Trade Practices Reports, different years.

it second only to Israel as the largest recipient of American aid. Over the period 1990–96 alone, cumulative aid to Egypt was $15.76 billion, which represents 26 percent of Egypt's GDP in 1995. Most of the aid (56 percent in 1996) was earmarked for military expen-

Figure 1-5. *Sectoral Distribution of U.S. FDI in Egypt, Mexico, and Israel, 1995*

Percent
100
80
60
40
20
0
Others
Manufacturing
Petroleum
Others
Manufacturing
Others
Manufacturing
Egypt
Mexico
Israel

Source: U.S. Department of State, Country Reports on Economic Policy and Trade Practices, 1996.

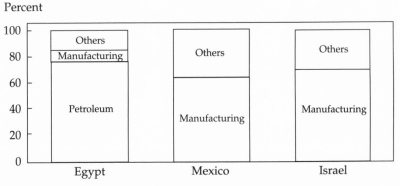

diture. The rest was in the form of grants (35 percent) and commodity export credit guarantees (9 percent) (figure 1-6).

Aid funds undoubtedly helped relax the foreign exchange constraint facing the Egyptian economy. Aid earmarked for military expenditure also benefited the economy, given that Egypt would have had to raise these funds itself, or a fraction of them, internally or externally. Moreover, aid has contributed to the expansion of infrastructure and helped to support policy and institutional reforms to encourage a more market-oriented and private sector–led economy. However, aid may have given policymakers a cushion that delayed essential policy reforms, as is said to have occurred in Korea, which only began its reform process in the early 1960s when the United States threatened to stop the flow of aid.[4] In addition, aid may have displaced domestic savings by making more resources available for consumption.[5]

Now that the future of U.S. aid to Egypt appears uncertain, alternative ways must be found to maintain economic ties between Egypt and the United States. One alternative is an FTA, which is likely to succeed if it is designed to satisfy the interests of both parties.

Figure 1-6. *Components of U.S. Aid to Egypt, 1996*
Percent except as noted

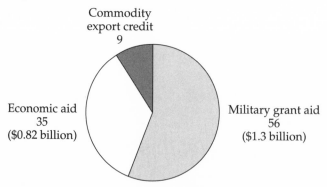

Commodity
export credit
9

Economic aid
35
($0.82 billion)

Military grant aid
56
($1.3 billion)

Source: U.S. Embassy, *Foreign Economic Trends and Their Implications for the United States,* various issues.

Highlights of the Book

In chapter 2 Ahmed Galal and Sahar Tohamy examine the choices negotiators face and the probable impact of the most likely FTA scenario for Egypt. They consider three broad choices: an agreement of the U.S.-Israeli type, which focuses on eliminating industrial tariffs and border restrictions; a deeper agreement along the lines of NAFTA, which includes services, foreign investment, and rules on behind-the-border obstacles presented by standards, government procurement, and regulatory practices and thus can be thought of as a WTO-plus arrangement; or a mix of both. Galal and Tohamy argue that a mix is probable and desirable from an Egyptian perspective. For one thing, it would enable Egypt to avoid adopting U.S. environmental and labor standard policies, which may not be appropriate at its current level of development. For another, it would give Egypt access to U.S. markets (especially for textile and agricultural products) and increased FDI, and it would improve impressions of the country's policy reform in the international community. Furthermore, the Egyptian economy is ready for an FTA with the United States, although the FTA itself could foster further reform.

In chapter 3, Robert Lawrence looks at the situation from the U.S. perspective. The United States, he argues, will probably adhere to a NAFTA-style (WTO-plus) agreement because current U.S. trade policy emphasizes deeper international integration; the United States uses a multitrack rather than a purely multilateral approach to trade liberalization; trade policy is highly politicized within the United States; and there are domestic concerns about the impact of globalization on unskilled American workers. Lawrence concludes that an FTA with Egypt will be beneficial to the United States, though its impact will be relatively small, particularly on U.S. employment. But it would improve access to Egyptian markets and would benefit the U.S. consumer, especially in textiles and clothing. Fostering economic development in Egypt would also serve an important U.S. foreign policy aim in the Middle East, namely, peace and stability.

Bernard Hoekman, Denise Konan, and Keith Maskus round out the discussion in chapter 4 with an assessment of the economic impact on the Egyptian economy if Egypt were to sign an FTA with the United States on top of its agreements with the European Union and the countries of the Arab League. In their estimate, a classical FTA with the United States would create trade between $252 million and $342 million and reduce trade diversion from other sources by $233 million to $197 million. A broader Egypt-U.S. (WTO-plus) FTA, entailing the elimination of nontariff barriers, would further increase the calculated gains in trade to $450 million and reduce the losses associated with trade diversion to $170 million. The net trade benefit of EU, Arab, and U.S. agreements is therefore positive, though a WTO-plus FTA would bring bigger gains, thanks to a reduction in the cost of nontariff barriers and bureaucratic constraints.

The bottom line, according to all three chapters, is that an FTA between Egypt and the United States is the logical next step for both countries if their economic relationship is to be sustainable and mutually beneficial. For the United States, the economic benefits and employment effects will be small but positive. The main benefits will be political in nature, in that a growing and stable Egypt is good for peace in the region. Moreover, it will have positive spillover effects on neighboring countries and thereby secure the constant flow of oil. For Egypt, the benefits from access to U.S. markets are also modest, but the potential gains in FDI and domestic reforms could be significant. However, although the net gains from increased and improved access, investment, and reform credibility are admittedly difficult to quantify, they could be significant. Thus, an FTA with the United States may well be the next building block toward full liberalization for Egypt, inasmuch as the United States is Egypt's second trading partner after the European Union. Such an agreement will also certainly reduce trade and investment diversion resulting from the treaty about to be signed with the European Union and that already has been signed with the Arab countries.

Concluding Remarks

Beyond Egypt and the United States, the analysis has broad implications for countries contemplating regional agreements. The foremost is that "deeper" FTAs are better for reforming economies than "shallow" FTAs. Deeper, WTO-plus FTAs bring about reforms of domestic policies and regulations that reduce transaction costs and induce investment. However, deeper does not always mean better. It is beneficial to internationalize domestic regulatory reforms only if the reforms entail policies that are compatible with the needs and preferences of the developing countries. Great care must be taken to ensure that the commitments in the agreement do in fact enhance welfare in developing nations.

Notes

1. Bhagwati (1993).
2. Subramanian (1997).
3. The potential implications of such an agreement for the Egyptian economy have been analyzed in Galal and Hoekman (1997b).
4. Krueger (1997).
5. Burnside and Dollar (1997).

CHAPTER TWO

Toward an Egypt-U.S. Free Trade Agreement

An Egyptian Perspective

Ahmed Galal and Sahar Tohamy

MOUNTING EVIDENCE suggests that openness is essential to economic growth.[1] This premise is being translated into actions the world over, from Latin America to the Far East. Simultaneously, more and more developed and developing countries are forming regional trading blocs, the most well known of which are the European Union (EU), the North American Free Trade Agreement (NAFTA), the ASEAN Free Trade Agreement (AFTA), and Mercosur (of South America). Regional trading blocs have been pursued to secure market access, attract international capital, and anchor policy reforms.

Like other countries, Egypt has been moving ahead on both fronts. Since the early 1990s, it has taken significant steps to liberalize the trade regime. Most notably, it has unified the exchange rate and devalued the currency, removed quantitative restrictions, and lowered tariff barriers. On the regional front, Egypt is about to conclude a free trade agreement with the European Union. At the same time, major efforts are under way to implement the FTA with Arab countries. And, in their April 1997 meeting, President Hosni Mubarak and Vice President Al Gore agreed to explore the possibility of an FTA between Egypt and the United States.

The Egyptian and American teams meeting to discuss an FTA

between their respective countries are likely to have several leading questions on their minds. What is in it for each party? What terms will benefit both parties? And how will each of them reconcile the agreement with other international commitments? This chapter explores these questions from an Egyptian perspective.

An underlying assumption of the analysis is that the economic relationship between Egypt and the United States has several distinctive features. First, it does not rest on economic grounds alone. Political factors play an important role, as evidenced by the magnitude of U.S. aid to Egypt ($2.3 billion annually). Second, both sides are aware that the case for continued economic aid may weaken in the future. At the same time, the United States will continue to be interested in supporting Egypt because of its role in promoting peace in the region and in maintaining a stable Middle East, both of which are important in their own right and essential for the secure flow of oil from the region. Third, whether or not aid to Egypt diminishes in the future, the United States and Egypt need to see trade and investment as beneficial to both parties. Otherwise opposition will slow levels of activity in these areas.

The rest of this chapter opens with an outline of the broad choices faced by negotiators on both sides. It next turns to the likely terms of an agreement and the potential benefits to Egypt, especially if the Egyptian economy stands ready to respond.

Broad FTA Choices

Within the limits of international commitments and domestic politics, the United States and Egypt can opt for "shallow" or "deep" integration.[2] They can focus on trade, services, and investment, or a subset of these; or they can follow the provisions of the General Agreement on Tariffs and Trade (GATT) or go beyond by harmonizing their domestic regulatory policies. The economic impact of the agreement for both parties will depend on which course they choose. Two questions are of interest here. First, what are the broad types of FTAs? Second, which types are the negotiators likely to seek?

Three broad types of FTAs come to mind. The first is a *classical free trade agreement*, along the lines of the U.S.-Israel FTA. This type of agreement focuses on eliminating tariffs and quantitative restrictions among the parties concerned. It usually gives little attention to harmonizing domestic competition policies and regulations that may influence investment and trade flows as much as border policies, if not more so. While they may be perceived as a step in the direction of multilateral liberalization, border-liberalization trade agreements represent "incomplete" efforts toward regional integration and an efficient allocation of resources.

One economic effect of classical free trade agreements is to "create" trade between the partners of the agreement and hence increase the welfare of the nations involved.[3] At the same time, they "divert" trade between the countries involved, on the one hand, and the rest of the world, on the other. The net effect can be positive or negative, but is generally limited in magnitude. Egypt's gain from trade liberalization with the European Union, for example, is expected to amount to approximately 0.2 percent of GDP.[4] Another free trade agreement with the United States is likely to reduce trade diversion, given the relative importance of the United States as a trading partner to Egypt.

The second broad choice negotiators may consider is a *deep integration agreement*, of the variety adopted in NAFTA. Agreements of this type extend liberalization to many aspects of the domestic economic environment affecting the production of goods, services, and investment. They endeavor to harmonize competition policies and regulatory institutions in matters such as environmental standards, labor laws, government procurement, antitrust legislation, and intellectual property rights. Such agreements come closest to completely eliminating barriers to trade and capital flows. The recent vintage of FTAs falls in this category.

The advantage of deep integration agreements is that they can generate both static and dynamic gains. Static gains follow from a better allocation of resources in a more liberalized environment.

Dynamic gains follow from greater investment, improved productivity, and reduced transaction costs. To the extent that they also enhance investor confidence in the stability of policy reform, they reduce the perception of risk and encourage the flow of foreign direct investment (FDI). In turn, FDI can produce an immediate increase in labor productivity and a more long-term accumulation of technology and human capital.

Deeper integration does not always mean better integration, however. At times, common standards may favor industries of one country at the expense of those in another. It is also possible that forcing the regulatory policy of one country on another may serve as an indirect trade barrier.[5] Furthermore, not all countries are at the same level of development. As a result, immediate enforcement of the agreement may discriminate against the local industry of the poorer country, depriving its producers of the ability to adjust and take the necessary steps to compete against large, well-established multinational industries.

Faced with the limitations of classical and deep free trade agreements, the negotiators may opt for a combination of both. This hybrid can be termed an *eclectic free trade agreement*. It seeks both to liberalize the trade barriers between the two parties and to harmonize *some* domestic competition policies and regulatory institutions. Which domestic policies a country chooses to negotiate and harmonize must be determined on a case-by-case basis, in view of the extent to which domestic regulatory policies and institutions diverge among the parties involved and the extent to which it is politically feasible to bridge the gap.

Because this type of agreement cannot be well defined up front, its effect cannot be easily predicted. However, it is reasonable to expect a well-designed eclectic FTA to be more beneficial than the other two types of agreements: not only can it generate the static and dynamic gains associated with deep integration agreements, but it can also avoid the shortcomings of deep integration agreements associated with the imposition of inappropriate regulatory policy of one country on another. Conversely, a poorly designed eclectic FTA can have a deleterious effect.

Terms of the Agreement and Potential Benefits to Egypt

Assuming that the negotiators come to the conclusion that an eclectic FTA is both desirable and feasible, what terms are they likely to agree on? What are the likely benefits to Egypt in this case? Both questions are best discussed in relation to market access, investment, and policy reform.

Market Access

The performance of Egypt's nontraditional exports has been less than satisfactory in recent years. During the period 1984–93, manufacturing exports grew at the modest rate of 1.0 percent per year.[6] This poor performance is attributed to several factors, one of which is market access. Therefore an important question to consider is whether an FTA with the United States will give Egyptian exporters greater access to the U.S. market.

The short answer is that the agreement is likely to include provisions to that effect. Both NAFTA and, to a lesser extent, the 1985 U.S.-Israel FTA contains articles that provide for the elimination of nontariff restrictions and the elimination or reduction of tariffs between partners. The two agreements also involved complementary provisions in areas such as quality control, antidumping regulations, and requirements for the purchase of local goods. An FTA with Egypt is likely to do the same. The question is: will these provisions increase market access by Egyptian exporters to the U.S. market?

According to the most favored nation (MFN) schedule, the American economy is fairly open, with an average tariff rate of 5.9 percent (table 2-1). Although this suggests limited increased access to the U.S. market, such may not be the case. Egyptian exporters face high tariffs on important exports to the United States, notably textiles and agricultural products. Under the MFN tariff schedule, U.S. textile imports face an average tariff of 10.5 percent, and a maximum tariff of 35 percent. In addition, exports of textiles to the United States are subject to country quotas. Egypt

Table 2-1. U.S. Most Favored Nation Tariffs in 1995 by Two-Digit
International Standard for Industrial Classification

	Applied tariff in 1995			
	Minimum tariff	Maximum tariff	Average tariff	Number of non-ad valorem
Agriculture	0	188	4.1	203
Agriculture, hunting	0	188	5.4	194
Forestry, logging	0	10	1.0	3
Fishing	0	8	0.5	6
Manufacturing	0	151	6.1	1,193
Food and beverages	0	151	8.7	541
Tobacco products				11
Textiles	0	35	10.5	62
Wearing apparel	0	34	12.9	79
Luggage and handbags	0	48	11.6	16
Wood and wood products	0	18	3.8	12
Paper and paper products	0	15	2.0	2
Publishing and printing	0	7	1.7	10
Coke and refined petrol	0	7	1.7	9
Chemicals and chemical products	0	22	5.0	173
Rubber and plastic products	0	15	4.4	1
Other nonmetal mineral products	0	38	6.9	18
Basic metals	0	18	4.3	12
Fabricated metal products	0	16	4.3	57
Machines and equipment	0	13	3.0	5
Office machines	0	5	1.9	0
Electrical machines	0	23	4.1	0
Radio and TV equipment	0	15	4.7	0
Medical and precision instruments	0	19	5.0	152
Motor vehicles and trailers	0	25	3.1	0
Other transport equipment	0	18	4.2	0
Furniture, jewelry, toys	0	32	4.4	33
Overall	0	188	5.9	1,441

Source: Inter-American Development Bank, Statistics and Quantitative Analysis,
Integration and Regional Programs Department.

faces quotas on eighteen textile products, including cotton yarn, cloth, and various types of ready-made garments and clothing. Furthermore, under the Uruguay Round the United States is only committed to reducing its trade-weighted average tariff on textiles from 17.2 percent to 15.2 percent over ten years. Without an FTA, Egyptian exporters will therefore continue to face tariff barriers to the U.S. market (table 2-2).

In the agricultural sector, Egypt faces tariffs as high as 188 percent on specific commodities, plus various non–ad valorem duties.[7] Although it does not have to contend with quotas on agricultural exports to the United States, the current MFN tariff schedule and the U.S. commitments under the Uruguay Round do not eliminate tariffs on agricultural products. In fact, the United States is committed to reducing existing tariffs by 36 percent on average over a period of six years (table 2-2). Accordingly, an FTA with the United States that includes immediate access for agricultural products of Egyptian origin will increase Egypt's exports.

Such access would be consistent with the U.S. agreement in the context of NAFTA, whereby it is expected to eliminate immediately all nontariff barriers to agricultural trade, generally through their conversion to either "tariff-rate quotas" or ordinary tariffs. Above-quota trade will be subject to the gradual reduction of tariffs. All tariff barriers between Mexico and the United States will be eliminated no later than ten to fifteen years after the signing of NAFTA.[8] If the United States agrees to similar terms with Egypt, they may prove to be particularly important, since the proposed Egypt-EU agreement does not include a substantial increase in access to the EU markets.

As for timing, Egypt is expected to have almost immediate access to the U.S. market, while American firms will have delayed access to the Egyptian market. This parallels the treatment of Mexico in the context of NAFTA, in which the opening of U.S. borders to most of Mexico's manufactures was implemented immediately, while the elimination of Mexican tariffs is phased over a period of five to ten years. A similar asymmetric timetable would be followed in the proposed Egypt-EU agreement. Additional

Table 2-2. *Selected U.S. Commitments under the GATT*

Agreement	U.S. commitment
General Agreement on Tariffs and Trade (GATT)	1. Eliminates tariffs in sectors such as construction, agricultural and medical equipment, steel, pharmaceuticals, paper, pulp and printed material, and furniture and toys.
	2. Reduces trade-weighted tariff averages on industrial products by 35 percent.
	3. Increases the number of 'bound' tariff lines to 100 percent.
	4. Requires participation in a tariff harmonization initiative that reduces tariffs in the chemical sector to very low rates reaching zero in some cases.
Agreement on Agriculture[a]	5. Replaces nontariff barriers (NTB) with tariffs.
	6. Reduces new and existing tariffs by 36 percent on average over six years.
	7. Curtails export subsidies in budgetary outlays by 36 percent.
	8. Reduces domestic support to agricultural producers by 20 percent over six years.
Agreement on Textiles and Clothing	9. Reduces tariffs on textiles and apparel from a 17.2 percent to a 15.2 percent trade-weighted ad valorem average over ten years.
	10. Increases the Multifiber Agreement quota growth rates in three successive stages over ten years: 16 percent in 1995, an additional 25 percent in 1998, and an additional 27 percent in 2002.

Source: GATT Secretariat, *The Results of the Uruguay Round of Multilateral Trade Negotiations* (1994) and Office of Textiles and Apparel, U.S. Department of Commerce.
a. Agriculture includes food processing.

provisions may be adopted to allow some "infant industries" in Egypt to receive above-agreement protection for a specific period of time. Such protection, however, is usually governed closely by the explicit terms of the agreement or by the supervisory body responsible for the administration of the terms of the agreement. Moreover, the parties are likely to agree on certain rules of origin to ensure that benefits of the agreement are accorded only to goods produced in the two countries. NAFTA, for example, specifies that textiles must abide by "yarn-forward" rules of origin and that automotive goods must contain 60 percent and 62.5 percent of North American content.

Under an FTA with the United States, Egyptian exporters may find increased access difficult to gain without hard negotiations regarding such issues as government procurement and domestic competition policy. In particular, the United States is likely to insist that Egypt eliminate the preferential access to government purchases given to Egyptian domestic suppliers (15 percent). The United States is also likely to demand that Egypt adopt antitrust legislation to prevent any abuse of market power and harmful mergers and acquisitions. These two issues are now being considered unilaterally by the Egyptian government in its effort to move toward a more market-oriented economy.

How much more trade can be expected under an FTA with the United States, assuming the agreements with the European Union and Arab countries are in force? It has been estimated that trade will increase by $342 million under a classical FTA and by $450 million under a NAFTA-like agreement.[9] A NAFTA-like agreement is also expected to cause less trade diversion ($170 million) than a classical FTA ($197 million). Overall, an FTA with the United States, in addition to the FTAs with the European Union and Arab countries, will likely increase welfare in Egypt by 1.26 percent of GDP in the classical case and 1.84 percent of GDP in the NAFTA-like case.

Investment

Egypt is eager to attract FDI in part because it wants to acquire new technology, as well as management and marketing capabilities. More important, perhaps, FDI would enable the country to grow much faster (7–8 percent) and thereby create enough jobs for new entrants into the labor market (estimated at half a million a year), while also reducing the current unemployment rate (which is in excess of 10 percent). If this high-growth scenario is to become a reality, the ratio of investment to GDP must be increased to 25–27 percent, yet national savings at present amount to only 18 percent. To the extent that the agreement will contribute to increased FDI in Egypt, the benefits to the economy could be substantial.

Here, the negotiators have a choice of two approaches. First, they can limit their commitments to those already made under GATT and GATS, which is what Egypt has done in its negotiation of the EU FTA. This approach was taken by Israel in its FTA with the United States.[10] Second, they can follow NAFTA, which goes significantly beyond GATT and GATS, and pursue investment liberalization by granting investors of the other country the right of establishment, eliminating performance requirements (for example, minimum exports, local contents, local presence for the provision of services), removing restrictions on currency expatriation, prohibiting the expropriation of foreign investment, and providing for fair compensation in case of expropriation. Like Mexico, they can also agree to allow foreign investment in most sectors of the economy, except those that are constitutionally reserved for the state, such as social services and maritime services.

From an Egyptian perspective, no further commitments beyond the GATT may seem necessary under an FTA with the United States, because Egypt can pursue liberalization of investment and services unilaterally (as Mexico did, for example, with respect to its telecommunications sector, and as Egypt can claim it is actually doing now). However, this may not be desirable, because Egypt can improve foreign investors' perception of the credibility of its policy reform if it commits to an external binding with the United States (as discussed in the next section). In addition, this approach may not be feasible if the United States insists on applying the NAFTA model to any of its subsequent FTAs with other countries, including Egypt. Whatever framework is adopted, either of the parties may still put a number of FDI-related issues on the table. These issues include intellectual property rights (IPRs) and labor laws.

The FDI-related arguments in favor of protecting IPRs are straightforward: they encourage the flow of FDI in such sectors as computer software and pharmaceuticals, and they encourage the private sector to invest in research and development. In principle, this should not be a problem for Egypt, since it is both a market for and a producer of products that IPRs can protect. Moreover, Egypt's present law protects IPRs and provides national treatment for the products of other countries.[11] These commitments were reiterated in Egypt's signing of the WTO Trade-Related Intellectual Property Rights Agreement (TRIPs).

The catch, however, is that TRIPs provides for a transition period starting in 1995, during which pharmaceutical patents may be put in a "black box" for ten years by countries that did not previously grant patent protection (including Egypt). A similar time frame is required to obtain approval for the commercial marketing of patented products in developed countries. This means that both the positive and negative effects of TRIPs on the Egyptian pharmaceutical industry will first be felt by the year 2005, if Egypt made no further commitments in its EU agreement. In an FTA with the United States, however, Egypt will in all likelihood be asked to eliminate or shorten the ten-year transition period TRIPs allows. Debate over the issue of timing has been intense in Egypt, perhaps because of the concern about the negative impact this will have on the pharmaceutical industry, and on consumers as the price of pharmaceutical products increases. To the extent that these are valid concerns, it may be possible to resolve the conflict by estimating the potential cost involved and agreeing on some form of financial compensation.

As for the interaction between labor laws and FDI, it is generally accepted that, all things being equal, FDI will gravitate to countries in which labor is both skilled and relatively inexpensive. Segmented labor markets, poor training programs, and inflexible wage policies act as deterrents to FDI. In Egypt the market is somewhat segmented, with 35 percent of the labor force working in the public sector and having few incentives to improve their skills. Labor laws seem extremely rigid when it comes to hiring and firing; however, the picture is not as grim as it appears. According to surveys of the business sector, labor laws are not as binding as they seem.[12] Furthermore, real wages declined during the period 1982/83 to 1992/93, which suggests that the market is more flexible than it seems.[13] And the Egyptian labor force is fairly skilled, as is clear from the fact that 10 to 15 percent of the force work in nearby countries.

Although U.S. negotiators may express concern about the rights of workers, the Egyptian side is likely to assert that its laws guarantee reasonable standards for health and safety, ban child labor, and safeguard against discrimination. In the end, the two parties may agree to provisions similar to those included in NAFTA. The essence of these provisions is that no commitments can be made beyond some guiding principles, subject to each party's domestic law, without establishing common minimum standards. Thus the parties may agree to develop their own laws, regulations, procedures, and practices protecting the rights and interests of their respective work forces. These could cover minimum employment standards, the right to collective bargaining, and antidiscrimination measures, among others. As in NAFTA, procedures could be included for issuing complaints about violations of the agreement and financial penalties.

How much will FDI in Egypt increase under an FTA with the United States? This is a difficult question to answer, especially because FDI depends on a host of factors. But if the experience of other countries is any guide, the benefits can be substantial. In Mexico, for example, the stock of U.S. FDI more than doubled, from $9.4 billion in 1990, when NAFTA was first announced, to about $19 billion in 1996.[14] Mexico also attracted substantial investment from non-U.S. sources, which, combined with U.S. investment, generated $24 billion worth of FDI over a period of five years, or the equivalent of 10 percent of Mexico's GDP in 1990 (table 2-3).[15]

Similarly, Spain and Portugal received large inflows of FDI fol-

Table 2-3. *Pre- and Post-Agreement Foreign Direct Investment (FDI) Flows in Mexico, Portugal, and Spain*

	Mexico	*Portugal*	*Spain*
Average annual FDI flows			
Pre-agreement[a] (billion U.S.$)	0.8	0.16	1.68
Post-agreement[b] (billion U.S.$)	4.8	0.73	5.09
Cumulative FDI/ base-year GDP[c]			
Five-year (percent)	10	16.24	13.89
Ten-year (percent)	n.a.	59.58	45.16

Source: *International Financial Statistics,* various issues.
n.a. not available.
a. Pre-agreement averages are over years 1985–89 for Mexico and 1980–84 for Portugal and Spain.
b. Post-agreement averages are over years 1990–94 for Mexico and 1985–89 for Portugal and Spain.
c. Base year is 1990 for Mexico and 1985 for Portugal and Spain.

lowing their accession to the European Union in 1985. The average annual FDI flowing into Spain increased from $1.68 billion in the five years before integration to an average of $5.09 billion in the five years following integration. The corresponding figures for Portugal are $0.16 billion for 1980–84 versus $0.73 billion for 1985–89. Over a period of ten years, the two countries attracted FDI equivalent to about half their respective GDPs in 1985 (table 2-3).

The FTA as an Anchor for Policy Reform

Like Mexico, Egypt could use the FTA with the United States to further enhance the credibility of its reform effort, which has intensified since 1990. Without such an agreement, large foreign investors, especially those interested in asset-specific sectors in utilities, will either refrain from investing heavily in these sectors or will require a high-risk premium to do so. An agreement that liberalizes services can reduce this risk and attract capital at favorable terms. Risk will be reduced even further if foreign investors believe that the United States will support the Egyptian economy in the event of a crisis, as it did in the Mexican case.[16]

It can be argued, however, that Egypt's economic reforms have already gained the confidence of foreign investors, especially since 1996. This view is supported by the favorable rating Egypt recently received from Standard and Poor's and the International Bank Credit Agency (IBCA). The fact that Egypt is about to sign an agreement with the European Union might further reduce the merits of using an FTA with the United States as a policy anchor. In addition, some believe that an external agreement will weaken Egypt's control over domestic policies.

These arguments are not persuasive, however. For one thing, the history of reform in Egypt is too recent. Despite its favorable institutional rating, some investors may hesitate to become involved in Egypt. For another, the agreement with the European Union is somewhat limited, since it contains no commitments regarding the right of establishment or liberalization of services.[17] As a result, foreign investors may not view it as a serious mechanism, as they did NAFTA. The more difficult issue is the tension between national sovereignty and international commitments. This necessitates a trade-off, which cannot be dismissed lightly. Perhaps the most reasonable way to relieve this tension is not to forgo the benefits of using the FTA as a binding mechanism. Rather, negotiators should focus on reforms that are consistent with Egypt's reform strategy and should make sure that the agreement clearly spells out the terms for dealing with exceptional circumstances.

Potential FTA Benefits and the Responsiveness of the Egyptian Economy

The extent to which the potential benefits of an FTA with the United States are fully realized will depend on whether the Egyptian economy can fully exploit the opportunities offered by the agreement. Less than prudent macroeconomic management, institutional rigidities, and excessive protection of domestic markets all deter FDI, erode the ability of firms to export to a market as competitive as that in the United States, and provide incentives to sell domestically rather than abroad. Whether the economy is indeed ready to take advantage of an FTA with the United States can be determined by examining the reforms to date, the remaining weaknesses, and the way in which the agreement could promote further reform.

Reforms to Date

Since the 1980s the macroeconomic policy environment in Egypt has taken great strides toward building credibility, attracting FDI, and promoting exports.[18] That is not to say that the macroeconomic environment is problem-free, or that further reforms are not needed. Rather, things have improved significantly in the 1990s, and, according to some, the Egyptian stabilization program has proved to be one of the most successful in the developing world.[19] How did this occur?

With the assistance of the International Monetary Fund (IMF) and the World Bank, Egypt launched a major stabilization program in 1991 in the tradition of what is known as the Washington consensus. In particular, it took decisive action on the fiscal front, reducing the budget from more than 15 percent of GDP to 1.3 percent in 1994/95. In addition, the program unified the exchange rate and devalued the currency, tightened monetary policy, liberalized the interest rate, and decontrolled prices. In addition, 50 percent of Egypt's external debt was forgiven following the Gulf War.

The program produced remarkable results. Between 1990/91 and 1995/96, inflation declined from 21 percent to 7.1 percent. External debt fell from 84 percent of GDP in 1992 to 46 percent in GDP in 1996, and the current account remained in surplus for most of the period. Increased confidence in the Egyptian economy was seen in rapid de-dollarization, which went from about 50 percent in 1991/92 to about 24 percent in 1995/96. Moreover, the buildup of capital inflows increased reserves to $20 billion, which amounts to about nine years of current debt-servicing requirements. Although GDP growth slowed considerably during the reform period, it has shown signs of recovery in recent years. Real

GDP growth was 5.0 percent in 1996/97 and is expected to increase further in the next few years. By 1997 the cumulative effect of these reforms earned Egypt a rating of BBB- from Standard and Poor's and the IBCA.

But stabilization is only a precondition required to enable economic agents to respond flexibly to market challenges and opportunities. Without structural reforms to reduce transactions costs, enforce contracts efficiently, and restore flexibility in the labor and capital markets, the "right" prices may not be acted upon.[20] Here, too, the government has made significant progress, most notably in opening up the economy, reducing the role of the state, and developing the financial sector. Some reforms have been undertaken with the support of the IMF and World Bank, while others have been done unilaterally.

Egypt's trade liberalization started in 1991 with the removal of import bans and export controls. Progress continued with regular reductions of maximum and average tariff rates. As a result, the average tariff rate is now only 16 percent, with a maximum rate of 50 percent (except in the case of automobiles, cigarettes, and alcohol). Because tariffs are also imposed on imported intermediate inputs, effective rates of protection (ERPs) of domestic producers are lower than nominal rates, which declined from 13.1 percent in 1992 to 9.1 percent in 1996. (See the appendix for data sources and the details of our calculations). This more open trade regime has exposed firms to greater competition, thereby enhancing their capacity to respond more favorably to improved market access abroad.

In an attempt to reduce the role of the state, the government recently accelerated the privatization of state-owned enterprises (SOEs). In 1996/97 alone, it sold the majority of the shares of 40 companies out of some 300 SOEs. The government intends to complete the sale of the remaining two-thirds of public sector companies by 1998/99. In view of the experience of other countries, privatization is expected to improve efficiency, increase investment, and contribute to consumer welfare without hurting workers.[21] Since 1991 the government has simultaneously introduced major pieces of legislation to reduce taxation and eliminate exchange and credit controls.[22] Other laws have been passed to ease entry into the banking sector, including a bill enacted in 1996 that allows 100 percent foreign ownership of banks. A new investment law passed in 1997 unifies and simplifies the procedures for undertaking new investment and gives the private sector incentives to invest.

Significant reforms have also been undertaken within the financial sector. To begin with, government funds were used to compensate banks for earlier structural weaknesses and an overregulated financial sector. Subsequently, several policies were introduced to strengthen the banking sector and improve its ability to meet the needs and risks of a liberalized environment. Banks are now allowed to set their interest rates and service charges, and they can operate freely in local or foreign currencies. All but one of the joint-venture banks have been privatized, and the banking sector's involvement in corporate and consumer credit is growing.[23]

Helped by the privatization program, Egypt's efforts to strengthen the Egyptian stock exchange have paid off. Capitalization/GDP went up from 7 percent in 1991/92 to an estimated 24 percent in 1996/97. Yet some would argue that the stock market has grown at the expense of the banking sector.[24] Further liberalization of trade and investment could bring this trend to a halt; hence the importance of an FTA agreement that liberalizes trade and investment between Egypt and the United States. As the domestic sector responds to new investment and trade possibilities, competition between various sources of finance can guarantee improved allocation of resources, even if the banking sector itself is excluded from services liberalization.

In sum, the reforms to date appear to have prepared the Egyptian economy to enter an FTA with the United States. By contrast, such a proposal would have fallen on deaf ears or met with skepticism in the 1980s.

Remaining Weaknesses

Despite this progress, some weaknesses remain. The current account is expected to show a deficit in the next few years. Imports are likely to go up as further tariff reductions are made. And non-oil exports may not increase substantially because of the exchange rate policy and other domestic constraints. Over the past few years, non-oil exports hardly grew, and their contribution to GDP is a modest 3.5 percent. This ratio compares with 15 percent in Indonesia. An important reason for this poor performance is an overvalued exchange rate, which was at approximately 30 percent between July 1991 and December 1996.[25] Although receipts from services grew by 29 percent between 1991/92 and 1996/97, other services exports such as communications, media, shipping, engineering, and Arabic software remain virtually unexploited.

Another area of weakness is the low level of saving and investment. Investment accounts for approximately 17 percent of GDP, which is far below the level in dynamic export-oriented countries such as Indonesia (where it reached 37 percent in 1996). One reason for low savings is the large public sector: SOEs alone account for about 30 percent of GDP.[26] Another reason is the pay-as-you-go pension fund system, which provides pensioners limited incentives to save. Yet another important factor is the low level of FDI, which suggests that foreign investors consider Egypt less attractive than other emerging markets, notably in East Asia and Latin America.

Because savings, investment, and exports have been low, the economy has not grown fast enough to create sufficient jobs to absorb the growing labor force. Unemployment is currently running at about 10–13 percent.[27] Admittedly, the policy of guaranteed employment in the public sector succeeded in maintaining near full employment for decades, even if these jobs were not productive. But this policy proved unsustainable and left the economy with an unemployment challenge that is yet to be met.

The reforms on the agenda, in other words, are not close to being finished, if they ever will be. Further structural reforms are awaiting action. Indeed, evidence shows that if Egypt were to improve its economic and institutional environment to meet the standards prevailing in East Asia, the Egyptian GDP per capita could increase by as much as 6.3 percent.[28] A survey of the private sector suggests that the costs of red tape and other institutional constraints still burden business by as much as 15 percent.[29]

Readiness of the Economy and the FTA

The favorable economic environment and the weaknesses of the economy make an FTA with the United States attractive for Egypt. The environment is conducive to investment and exports and enables firms to take advantage of the opportunities offered by the agreement. And the weaknesses attest to the need for an FTA to reduce the saving-investment gap, penetrate new markets, and make reform more credible. Because work on the reform agenda is not yet finished, the FTA may also be used to support further reform. It could help specific industries as well, particularly in three export categories: textiles, agricultural products, and nontraditional products in which Egypt may have a comparative advantage. [30]

To judge by the revealed comparative advantage (RCA) of its exports to the United States, Egypt enjoys a comparative advantage in eight of ten HS two-digit textile sectors (table 2-4). Therefore, textiles show a fair degree of competitiveness in the U.S. market, despite the trade barriers there and the level of ERP in Egypt, which in 1996 was 31.5 percent for spinning and weaving and 40.7 percent for ready-made garments (table 2-5).[31] Accordingly, an FTA that ensures duty-free access of Egyptian textiles to the United States could be instrumental in promoting this sector.

By contrast, agricultural products have been experiencing increasingly negative ERPs since 1992 (table 2-5). Accordingly, greater access to markets abroad is likely to lead to a greater supply of these products. The problem is that agricultural products are usually subject to extensive quality and specification controls. In this atmosphere of negative protection, however, efforts to harmonize these procedures under an FTA are likely to help this sector penetrate the U.S. market.

Similarly, the future looks promising for many nontraditional oil industries, especially in view of the expected downward trend in ERP after the full implementation of the FTA with the European Union. It appears that only four of thirteen industries will remain positively protected by the year 2010.[32] These sectors will

Table 2-4. *Revealed Comparative Advantage for Egyptian Textiles, 1994*[a]

Percent

Textile	World	U.S.
Silk yarn and fabrics	–252	*
Wool yarn and fabrics	–239	602
Cotton yarn and fabrics	373	619
Other natural fiber yarns and fabrics	119	*
Manmade filament	–211	14
Manmade staple fibers	–252	–58
Wadding, felt and unwoven; yarn; twine; cordage	–19	*
Carpets and other textile floor coverings	311	731
Special woven fabrics; tufted textile fabrics; lace; tapestries	37	61
Impregnated, coated, laminated textile fabrics	–178	–137
Knitted or crocheted fabrics	4	*
Apparel and clothing accessories, knitted or crocheted	371	774
Apparel and clothing accessories, not knitted or crocheted	464	762
Other made-up textile articles; worn clothing	379	777

Sources: Calculated from CAPMAS trade data. RCA equation from Greenaway and Milner (1994).
*Ratio not defined.
a. RCA(%) = ln $((X_i/X)/(M_i/M))$ * 100 where X_i and M_i are sector i's exports and imports, respectively, while X and M are Egypt's total exports and imports. RCA>0 indicates the presence of comparative advantage. The higher the index the more successful the trade performance of the sector in question.

be able to compete effectively in a more open trade environment. Furthermore, they will benefit significantly from simplified and harmonized import and export procedures that represent trade barriers, especially to small exporters.

Concluding Remarks

Current debate over aid to Egypt suggests that an FTA between it and the United States may be the logical next step in their rela-

Table 2-5. *Protection in Egypt, 1992 and 1996*[a]

	1992		1996	
	Nominal tariff	ERP	Nominal tariff	ERP
Agricultural food products	6.0	0.1	3.3	−4.4
Agricultural nonfood products	4.5	−2.2	4.2	−2.3
Livestock	9.1	3.9	7.9	4.4
Oil and gas extracts	5.0	−9.9	5.0	−12.2
Other extracts	8.3	−6.6	8.0	−7.4
Food processing	7.5	2.4	7.2	3.1
Cotton ginning	7.5	2.5	7.5	2.8
Spinning and weaving	44.6	47.9	31.1	31.5
Ready-made garments	99.3	82.6	54.4	40.7
Leather products (less footwear)	22.5	32.0	21.6	31.0
Footwear	83.0	73.2	53.6	42.2
Wood products (less furniture)	9.1	−15.0	8.8	−11.2
Furniture	87.8	105.9	48.2	53.8
Paper and printing	16.0	12.6	17.8	15.3
Chemical products (less oil refining)	12.7	6.6	11.4	5.7
Oil refining products	9.4	6.0	9.4	6.0
Rubber and plastic products	17.0	6.6	14.7	5.3
Porcelain products	29.3	20.6	26.3	17.4
Glass products	40.5	32.0	32.0	23.8
Nonmetallic products	40.5	39.9	17.7	12.8
Metals and iron products	13.6	18.5	13.0	17.9
Machinery and equipment	25.0	14.5	19.8	9.4
Transportation means	40.2	36.1	56.9	58.8
Other manufacturing industries	25.6	18.3	10.9	2.5
Weighted average	20.9	13.1	16.8	9.1

Source: Authors' calculations.
a. Beverages and tobacco are excluded because of their high nominal tariffs.

tionship. Besides producing immediate benefits, in the form of increased net trade and investment, a strong relationship between the two countries will help foster peace in the region.

Not all FTAs are equally beneficial, however. As this chapter has pointed out, probably the best option for Egypt is an eclectic FTA that liberalizes trade and harmonizes *some* domestic policies and regulations. Deeper FTA of the NAFTA type might infringe on national sovereignty and bring inappropriate policies and institutions to Egypt. Conversely, a shallow FTA, such as the U.S.-Israel agreement, may do little to promote investment, liberalize services, or provide an anchor for policy reform.

The time for negotiating an agreement with the United States is now. Egypt is about to conclude an agreement with the European Union and has signed an FTA with the Arab countries. Therefore an agreement with the United States would reduce trade diversion. Indeed, the Egyptian economy is ready to take advantage of an agreement with the United States, given the significant reforms undertaken in the 1990s. Whatever weakness remains in the economy, an FTA with the United States would undoubtedly be a helpful force.

Appendix: Effective Rate of Protection (ERP)

ERP measures the extent to which nominal tariffs protect domestic value added (VA). A positive ERP indicates that domestic VA is protected, while a negative ERP indicates that domestic VA is taxed. The effective rate of protection (ERP) for sector I was calculated as

$$ ERP_i = \frac{Tariff_i - \sum_{j \neq i} Tariff_j * a_j}{1 - a_i} * 100 $$

where a_j is the input share of sector j in the production of sector i, calculated from the 1991/92 input-output (IO) table for Egypt; and $tariff_i$ is the imports-weighted nominal tariff of sector i of the IO table.[33]

Data on merchandise imports were obtained from CAPMAS at the two-digit level of the HS classification. Tariffs applied in 1992 and 1996 were obtained from Presidential Decrees 351 (1986) and 38 (1994) and their amendments. Because the data on tariffs were more detailed than the data on imports, the eight-digit 1994 imports were used to derive weighted tariffs for the two-digit imports. The trade and tariff data were then regrouped to correspond to the sectors of the IO table. Because there are no tariffs on services and inefficient services impose a tax on manufacturing and agriculture, "tariff equivalents" (based on comparative efficiency indicators) were assumed for the different services categories of the IO table. For the financial sector, a comparison of the real financial spread in Egypt and the European Union suggested that an implicit tariff of 20 percent could be assumed for this sector. The same rate was applied to the insurance sector. A 50 percent tariff equivalent was assumed for the communication sector after comparing the number of employees per line in Egypt with the world average. Comparisons of the costs of shipping and loading yielded a 30 percent rate for shipping and warehousing. No tariff equivalents were assumed for the other services sectors.

Notes

The authors are grateful to Galal Amin and those who participated in the conference "Toward an Egypt-U.S. Free Trade Agreement" for helpful discussion and comments. An earlier version of this chapter was presented at a workshop held at the Brookings Institution on October 3, 1997. We thank Samiha Fawzy, Bernard Hoekman, Robert Lawrence, Arvind Subramanian, and the workshop participants for useful comments. Thanks also go to Amal Refaat for excellent research assistance, Joe Attia for his contribution to the calculation of ERP, and Marwa Kassem and Mai Farid for additional help with data.

1. See, for example, Barro (1991); Krueger (1997); Sachs and Warner (1995).
2. See Lawrence (1997b).
3. Viner (1950).
4. Maskus and Konan (1997).
5. Noll (1997).
6. Sachs (1996).
7. Non–ad valorem duties are custom duties that are specified in dollars or cents per unit of imported commodity and not in terms of the commodity's value.
8. In the 1985 U.S.-Israel FTA, quantitative restrictions other than tariffs were maintained in each country to suit their general agricultural policy considerations.
9. Hoekman, Konan, and Maskus (this volume).
10. The 1985 U.S.-Israel agreement limits its coverage of trade in services to

recommending that the parties minimize restrictions on the flow of services between the two nations and develop means for cooperating on this goal.

11. Subramanian and Abd-el-Latif (1997).

12. Galal (1996).

13. Radwan (forthcoming).

14. Bureau of Economic Analysis, *Survey of Current Business,* various issues; and International Financial Statistics capital accounts data.

15. Kehoe (1996) argues that an important aspect of Mexico's liberalization is the removal of barriers to FDI.

16. For elaboration of the role of the United States in the Mexican crisis and the favorable effect of NAFTA as a policy anchor for Mexico, see Francois (1997).

17. Hoekman and Djankov (1997b).

18. On the importance of macroeconomic variables for FDI, see, for example, United Nations Center on Transnational Corporations (1993); Bajo-Rubio and Sosvilla-Rivero (1994); and Haddad and Harrison (1993).

19. Subramanian (1997).

20. Benham (1997).

21. Galal and others (1994).

22. The marginal tax rate was reduced from 65 percent to 48 percent, while the corporate rate was reduced to 42 percent and 34 percent for manufacturing.

23. The health of the banking sector is reflected in the improved profitability, the limited spread between borrowing and lending rates (3.8 percent in 1995/96), and the smaller exposure of banks to public companies' debt (the share of public sector credit in 1996 was 57 percent, which was down from 71 percent).

24. Subramanian (1997).

25. Subramanian (1997). Egypt uses the exchange rate as a nominal anchor.

26. Sachs (1996).

27. Fergany (1994).

28. Sachs (1996).

29. IBCA (1997). See also World Bank (1992, 1994).

30. Under the nontraditionally comparative advantage sectors we group all manufacturing sectors except food processing, textiles, minerals, and oil refining.

31. ERP calculations do not take into account the effect of the ban on imports of ready-made garments. Therefore the ready-made garment industry is necessarily more protected than the ERP figures suggest.

32. Galal and Hoekman (1997a).

33. For the derivation of ERP, see Hoekman and Djankov (1997a).

CHAPTER THREE

Toward an Egypt-U.S. Free Trade Agreement

A U.S. Perspective

Robert Z. Lawrence

FOR MANY AMERICANS, the idea of a free trade agreement between the United States and Egypt is surprising. Although they are fully aware that Egypt is strategically important as a partner in the search for peace and security in the Middle East, they tend to see it as a recipient of aid rather than an opportunity for trade. Since 1975, the U.S. government has spent more than $17.5 billion on economic assistance to Egypt in addition to $20 billion on military assistance.[1]

The U.S. view is quite understandable. In the 1980s, the Egyptian economy stagnated, and although Egypt's earlier growth had been rapid, it occurred behind doors that were virtually closed to the outside world. Furthermore, this was a state-controlled and protected economy that allowed Egypt's private entrepreneurs, not to mention foreign investors, to play only a limited role. As a result, selling and investing in Egypt has not been easy for American firms. Over the years, reports of the U.S. government have identified many impediments, including official policies such as import licensing, high tariffs, time-consuming and expensive customs and quality control procedures, and unofficial practices that in some cases reflected corruption (see the appendix to this chapter).

Another reason for Egypt's low economic profile has been developments elsewhere. While Egypt and other developing countries in the Middle East were still debating whether to adopt reforms, many emerging economies in other parts of the world were on the move. Global investors have had their attention riveted on nations in Asia, Latin America, and Eastern Europe that have dramatically reoriented their economies with outward-looking strategies.

In 1991, however, economic reform in Egypt began in earnest with the signing of an International Monetary Fund agreement and Paris Club forgiveness of 50 percent of Egypt's official debt obligations. Since then, Egypt's macroeconomic stabilization record has been impressive. It has cut the budget deficit from 21 percent to 1.3 percent of GDP, reduced inflation from 25 to 7 percent, brought the current account into balance, and built foreign exchange reserves up to more than $20 billion. With the appointment of a new government in January 1996, Egypt committed itself to accelerated economic reform, privatization, liberalization, and a reduction of administrative bureaucracy. One indication of the seriousness of these intentions was its willingness to sign a free trade agreement with the European Union under the Euro-Med program, under which Egypt is scheduled to remove all trade barriers to European industrial products by 2010. In addition, an agreement has been reached among members of the Arab League to establish a free trade agreement over a ten-year period, starting in 1998.

These changes have also induced a shift in American policy. The U.S. aid program, which once mainly supported large public sector projects, is now designed principally to enhance private sector–led, export-oriented economic growth. Vice President Al Gore and President Hosni Mubarak have established collaborative groups of officials from the public and private sectors in both countries (the "Gore-Mubarak" partnership) to promote economic growth and job creation in Egypt and to strengthen economic and commercial ties between the two countries. The partnership seeks to maintain Egypt's momentum in creating a business environment favorable to investment by implementing policies that spur privatization, liberalize trade, develop a unified commercial law, create a dispute settlement process, and protect intellectual property rights.

Are these U.S. initiatives sufficient? Should the United States and Egypt deepen their economic relationship with a more comprehensive free trade agreement? From the U.S. perspective, these questions encompass several issues: What would be the impact of an agreement on the U.S. economy? Would it be effective in advancing U.S. economic interests in Egypt? How would it affect other U.S. trade policy initiatives and goals? Would it help promote broader U.S. interests in the Middle East? What terms are likely to be acceptable to the United States? Should the agreement mirror the relatively limited undertakings of the Euro-Med agreements or the U.S.-Israel FTA, or the more extensive undertakings of NAFTA or those planned for Free Trade Area in the Americas (FTAA)? To answer these questions, it is necessary to consider current U.S. trade strategy, the possibility of using other agreements as precedents (such as the U.S. Free Trade Agreement with Israel, Egypt's Euro-Med Partnership Agreement, NAFTA, and the FTAA), the impact of eliminating U.S.-Egyptian tariffs on trade and employment in the United States, and the options from a U.S. perspective.

The U.S. Trade Policy Context

An important aspect of our agenda is to build on the regional and multilateral agreements already reached, seeking higher levels of obligations. We also aim to expand the coverage of trade agreements to address practices that undermine benefits achieved through stronger trade rules and market access commitments: trade distortions created by low labor standards, excessive regulation, the lack of transparency, bribery and corruption, barriers to environmentally sustainable development and anti-competitive behavior affecting trade.[2]

The likelihood and character of a U.S.-Egypt FTA cannot be fully evaluated without taking into account several features of U.S. trade policy. In particular, the U.S. position in the world has changed over the postwar period and, in response, U.S. trade policy, which is highly responsive to domestic political concerns, has done likewise. The United States has stopped relying exclusively on multilateralism to deal with border barriers and has moved toward a multitrack strategy that focuses on deeper international economic integration. If a U.S.-Egypt free trade agreement is to prove attractive to the United States, it will have to mesh with these broader policy concerns.

For much of the postwar era, the United States has concentrated on supporting a rules-based, multilateral global system based on the General Agreement on Tariffs and Trade. With the decline in border barriers, however, the United States has begun calling for international measures for policies formerly thought of as purely domestic in nature and for governance mechanisms that make such measures more credible and binding. Product standards, investment policies, competition policies, intellectual property, environmental policies, labor standards, and human rights—all once thought of as matters of purely domestic concern—are coming under international scrutiny.

What accounts for this shift? In part, it is due to the changing nature of international competition, particularly, the complementary role that trade and direct foreign investment are increasingly called upon to play. To compete effectively in sophisticated, high-technology manufactured products, a significant domestic presence is often required for marketing, sales, and service. The ability to follow market trends, respond to customer needs, and acquire innovative smaller firms in all major markets has become essential for competitive success. Foreign investment and trade have increased not only in goods production but also in services, where FDI has grown even more rapidly. This is quite natural, since the distinctive feature of a service is that it is produced and consumed in the same location. The investment in services is being stimulated, in part, by the globalization of sectors once purely or heavily domestic in nature. The international diffusion of innovations has also become increasingly rapid.

These factors all lead firms to place greater emphasis on market access, as well as products. This development in turn causes frictions to arise among differing systems of corporate governance and rules of operation. Even where border barriers are removed, the weak enforcement of antitrust policies, for example, can lead to collusion, which limits new entry. Multinational firms that plan to produce components in one country and sell in others naturally seek secure operating rules, intellectual property rights, and technical standards and regulations that are internationally compatible.

Over the postwar period, trade has become more important to the U.S. economy, and U.S. firms have come under increasing competitive pressures. These changed circumstances have also had a profound impact on the degree of political importance accorded trade. The Constitution of the United States actually gives the Congress, rather than the president, the final say in the conduct of U.S. trade policy. And it is a power that the Congress jealously guards. As long as there was a strong domestic consensus in support of free trade and trade was relatively unimportant to most Americans, U.S. trade policy could remain focused more or less on global systemic goals, and U.S. trade policymaking could be confined to a handful of specialists. As trade pressures increased and trade became more salient in the domestic political debate, however, the conduct of U.S. trade policy became increasingly constrained by domestic political interests.

The growth in the political importance of trade issues has had three marked effects. First, it has increased the pressure on the U.S. administration to do something about them. Accordingly, U.S. policy has begun placing less emphasis on time-consuming multilateral endeavors, through the GATT, and more on multitrack strategies that combine unilateral, bilateral, and regional measures. Second, U.S. policy has become increasingly concerned with issues of fair trade. As national differences narrow and the intensity of competition increases, locational decisions become more sensitive to relatively small differences in domestic policies and practices. Paradoxically, the more similar countries are, the more significant their remaining differences become in determining trade and investment flows. This naturally puts pressure on countries to harmonize domestic rules and policies and to create "a level playing field."

With the increased politicization of trade policy, more attention is being given to noneconomic factors. When the members of Congress are asked to grant extensive trade benefits to trading partners, they use the opportunity to raise questions about issues such as human and animal rights, racial discrimination, and political practices. All these concerns have become intertwined in trade policy discussions.

An additional factor to note in the U.S. economic environment is the performance of the labor market. For two decades, its performance has been less than satisfactory. Real wages have stagnated. Between 1973 and 1996, real hourly compensation rose by only 9 percent.

This slump in the growth of real earnings has been accompanied by a second ominous development: a dramatic increase in the inequality of earnings in relation to education and occupation. A clear pattern has emerged over the decade in this regard: the higher the level of education, the higher the increase in earnings. The premium commanded by both men and women with higher educational or occupational status has increased sharply. The growing concern in the United States is that trade and international investment are creating a shift in the demand for unskilled labor. In view of the fact that the changes in the country's international economic relations coincide with slow real wage growth and widening wage inequality, it is easy to see why the former has frequently been advanced as a primary cause of the latter.

The debate over NAFTA in 1993 crystallized wage concerns that are perhaps best captured by Ross Perot's allusion to the "giant sucking sound" of jobs as they move southward. NAFTA has also been blamed for what many in the United States see as a major phenomenon: that of "runaway plants," which refers to the relocation by multinationals to low-wage countries. Some further complained that competition with countries that do not respect labor standards could have an adverse effect on U.S. workers.[3]

Though NAFTA was passed by the U.S. Congress, it left deep political wounds, made all the worse by Mexico's financial crises. In this environment, the Clinton administration has found it difficult to obtain fast-track authority from the Congress to negotiate its proposed Free Trade Agreement with Chile and to participate in other regional and multilateral trade negotiations.

These concerns affect both the feasibility and the character of a future U.S.-Egypt agreement. In part, they suggest that any such agreement is likely to be deep and involve more than simply the removal of border barriers. Furthermore, it may run into political obstacles beyond those related specifically to U.S.-Egypt trade questions or the likely economic impact of the agreement. Rather, they would stem from the broader concerns surrounding globalization and its impact on domestic economic problems in the United States.

Possible Models for an Agreement

A U.S.-Egypt free trade agreement could be patterned on two models. The first is the traditional free trade agreement of the GATT type, as seen in the U.S.-Israel FTA and the Euro-Med agreements between the European Union and other countries in the Middle East and North Africa. The second model, which can be called a WTO-plus agreement, is represented by NAFTA and the current plans for Western Hemisphere free trade. Table 3-1 provides a comparative overview of these agreements. From a U.S. standpoint, one of these options is better suited to a U.S.-Egypt agreement than the other, as explained in the following sections.

Table 3-1. *Key Provisions of the Israel-U.S. FTA and NAFTA, and Proposed Scope of Negotiations of the FTAA*

Scope	U.S.-Israel FTA	FTAA	NAFTA
Tariff elimination/ reduction	Duties on most products were eliminated when the agreement went into effect. The remaining products were put on three lists for progressive reduction. Duties on products on List C were frozen until January 1990, when they started going down in stages and reached zero in January 1995. Some import licenses and quotas based on agricultural policies are still permitted.	Ensure that all tariff and specified nontariff barriers be phased out within ten years (limited product exceptions). Introduce provisions to enable smaller less-developed countries to negotiate special phase-out schedules on some products.	Duties on most products were eliminated when the agreement went into effect. Tariff on products in Lists C and C+ will be removed in ten and fifteen annual equal stages, respectively, beginning on January 1, 1994. Most import and export restrictions, in particular quotas and import licenses, are eliminated.
Rules of origin	The product must contain at least 35 percent local value added.	Provide for clear and predictable rules of origin.	Products must contain at least 50–60 percent regional value added (depending on the method of calculation). A working group is established to supervise the administration and application of rules of origin. Special rules are applied to specific products such as automobiles and textiles.

Customs procedures	Develop common customs procedures providing for advance rulings, certificates of origin, verification procedures, information exchange, common customs forms.	Develop common customs procedures providing for advance rulings, certificates of origin, verification procedures, information exchange, common customs forms.	Develop common customs procedures providing for certificate of origin, verification procedures, advance rulings, review and appeal of origin determinations and advance rulings, customs cooperation, and establishment of a working group.
Government procurement	The FTA expands the coverage of the GATT Government Procurement Code. The threshold of contracts opened to competition is lowered to $50,000. Offsets from U.S. firms only apply to contracts above $500,000.	Provide for effective liberalization of government procurement, reflecting the principles of transparency, nondiscrimination, and due process.	NAFTA extends coverage to many federal government agencies not covered by the code, closes previous exclusions such as construction and service contracts, and offset requirements are prohibited. The threshold of purchases covered is $50,000 for government departments or agencies and $250,000 for federal government enterprises. The threshold is higher ($250,000 and $8 million, respectively) for construction services.
Technical barriers and standards	Besides establishing general rules of nondiscrimination and transparency, the FTA sets up a special working group to consider unsolved difficulties arising in trade in agricultural products.	Establish mechanisms to facilitate the removal of specific technical barriers to trade. Introduce new disciplines on transparency and due process in domestic regulatory system reflecting the principles of good regulatory practice.	Sanitary or phytosanitary measures maintained or introduced by any NAFTA country are permitted provided they are not a disguised form of trade restriction and are based on scientific principles and a risk assessment. Where possible, NAFTA countries commit themselves to using international standards and working toward equivalent measures without reducing any country's chosen level of protection of human, animal, or plant life or health.

(table continues)

Table 3-1 (*continued*)

Scope	U.S.-Israel FTA	FTAA	NAFTA
Agriculture	Permits the parties to maintain import restrictions other than customs duties, such as quotas, fees, and licensing.		Parties agree to eliminate all nontariff barriers to trade and convert these to tariffs or TRQs. The operation of this provision is deferred in the case of sensitive products such as corn and dry bean exports to Mexico, orange juice and sugar exports to the United States, and dairy products, poultry, and egg exports to Canada. Export subsidies for agricultural products are discouraged and permitted, after consultation, only to non-NAFTA exports. A special safe-guard provision can be invoked in the first ten years of the agreement if agricultural imports exceed specified trigger levels.
Intellectual property		Provide for full implementation of the WTO agreement on trade-related aspects of intellectual property rights (TRIPs).	The agreement has an extensive set of provisions protecting patent, copyright and trademark rights, and providing for their effective enforcement. These provisions largely build on the WTO agreement on TRIPS.
Subsidies	Israel joined the GATT Subsidies Code as part of its commitment to the FTS and agreed to eliminate export subsidy programs.	Establish new disciplines on agricultural export subsidies.	

Safeguards and unfair trade remedies	Parties reserve their right to apply safeguard, antidumping, and countervailing duty law.	Provide for the reform of antidumping and countervailing duty measures.	Parties reserve their right to apply antidumping and countervailing duty law. A special dispute settlement and mechanism for review of antidumping and countervailing duty determinations is established.
Competition policies		Provide, as appropriate, for disciplines on the interaction between trade and competition policies.	Each country commits itself to maintaining laws regulating anticompetitive practices. In the case of state enterprises and domestic monopolies, these enterprises are not to discriminate against other NAFTA firms or citizens in buying or selling goods or services and are to follow normal commercial considerations in their contractual activities. A trilateral committee is to be created to review the relationship between competition laws and trade matters, including presumably trade remedy laws. A side accord commits the parties to attempting to negotiate new legal regimes on dumping, subsidies, and countervailing duties within two years of the implementation of the agreement.

(table continues)

Table 3-1 (*continued*)

Scope	U.S.-Israel FTA	FTAA	NAFTA
Services	The parties agree to develop means of cooperation on trade in services pursuant to the provisions of a declaration containing nonbinding principles.	Expand on WTO GATS disciplines by providing nondiscriminatory treatment with limited exceptions.	Both the national treatment and the MFN principles are adopted. No local presence is required to provide covered services. A number of reservations are entered with respect to which services are covered or not. With respect to licensing and certification of professionals, the agreement provides that entry requirements should be related solely to competence and endorses a qualified mutual recognition principle.
			The agreement recognizes the right to establishment with respect to banking, insurance, securities, and other financial services, and adopts the NT and MFN principles with respect to financial services generally. Mexico reserves the right to impose market share limits on foreign firms in the financial services sector during a transitional period expiring in the year 2000.
			The agreement also provides for temporary entry for business persons into any NAFTA country.

Investment	Requirements to export and purchase domestic goods and services will not be a condition for investment or for receiving investment incentives.	Both the national treatment and the MFN principles are adopted. Performance requirements of foreign investors are generally prohibited. Some reservations are registered with respect to particular sectors.
	Provide for the development of investor/state dispute settlement procedures.	
Institutional arrangements	A joint committee was established to oversee the implementation of the agreement, to hold consultations and establish working groups as necessary, and to review the Declaration on Services.	The agreement provides for the creation of a NAFTA trade commission, to be supported by a full-time secretariat, and complemented by various groups and committees.
Dispute settlement	Sets a dispute settlement mechanism, with a consultation stage, a special joint committee, and a final nonbinding panel body.	Dispute resolution mechanisms are included, where binational panels will adjudicate on disputes between two member countries of the NAFTA, with the third country reserving the option of either participating in the proceedings or pursuing its own process of consultation and dispute resolution. Where complaint procedures are open to a NAFTA country either under GATT or NAFTA, it is entitled to choose which regime it pursues its complaint under, except where the complaint pertains to health, safety, or environmental standards, where the respondent country can insist on dispute
	Develop procedures modeled on the WTO process.	

(table continues)

Table 3-1 (*continued*)

Scope	U.S.-Israel FTA	FTAA	NAFTA
			resolution under NAFTA. In this respect, NAFTA provides for the creation of scientific boards to provide expert evidence to panels adjudicating on questions pertaining to health, safety, and environmental standards.
Infant industries	Permits for the purpose of protecting infant industries to increase or reintroduce import duties not exceeding 20 percent above the agreed level and 10 percent of total imports. That measure will be gradually abolished from January 1, 1995.		
Side accords on environmental and labor standards			Side accords set up an elaborate institutional machinery to ensure that existing environmental and labor laws in each of the three countries are effectively enforced with the possibility of fines and trade sanctions as penalties of non-compliance. The accords also provide for consultative mechanisms designed to promote a higher degree of harmonization of standards in these areas in the future.

U.S.-Israel Free Trade

The United States and Israel signed a free trade agreement for several reasons. An immediate concern for Israel was that the Generalized System of Preferences (GSP) giving Israel preferential access to the U.S. market was scheduled to expire in 1985. There was also a strong drive in the United States to restrict the program to the least developed countries and to force more advanced developing countries to "graduate" from it. Israel could have been among this group.[4]

What is perhaps surprising is that the United States was even willing to sign the agreement. It had been strongly opposed to preferential arrangements in the past, especially after having been the victim of such arrangements—particularly imperial preferences—in the 1930s. In addition, it had played a pivotal role in promoting the multilateral trading system. In the early 1980s, however, difficulties in launching the Uruguay Round led the United States to look more favorably on a multitrack approach to liberalization. Paradoxically, the fact that unique strategic arguments could be used to achieve an agreement with a partner that was not particularly significant economically helped reduce the political obstacles. Once concluded, it created a precedent that smoothed the way for the U.S.-Canada agreement.

Interestingly, as in the case of Egypt, Israel had already concluded a free trade agreement with the European Community (in 1975). That agreement was scheduled to be fully implemented by 1985, by which time Israeli tariffs on European exports were to be eliminated. Without a similar agreement with the United States, Israel would have been discriminating against its most important ally. This would have been politically problematic and economically damaging both to the United States, which would have suffered export losses, and to Israel, which would have had to purchase European products when American products would have been preferred, had they been available without import duties.

For the United States, the agreement created almost no need for adjustment, since more than 90 percent of Israeli exports were already entering the United States duty-free before the agreement was signed, under the GSP. Moreover, Israeli trade is relatively unimportant for the United States. U.S. exports to Israel, on the other hand, were subject to more significant tariff and nontariff barriers. In 1984 the explicit duties averaged about 3.8 percent, although additional fees (hidden tariffs) valued at 6.8 percent were also levied in the course of applying the TAMA, or purchase tax. From a mercantalist perspective, according to which exports are good and imports are bad, the agreement was likely to increase net exports for the United States. However, Israel had already agreed to give EU products duty-free access, so that Israeli producers were bound to make adjustments.

Tariffs were reduced in four stages over a ten-year period. In the first stage tariffs were eliminated on 8 percent of U.S. exports to Israel and 53 percent of Israel's exports to the United States. Israel, as the relatively less developed partner, was given more time to phase in its concessions.

The agreement apparently met the basic requirements of GATT Article 24, which governs preferential trading agreements. It covered substantially all trade, it did not raise external barriers, and it was implemented within ten years. However, it did not go beyond GATT by implementing measures that would have achieved deeper economic integration. First, the agreement did not eliminate trade remedies, that is, countervailing duties and antidumping.[5] And it did not implement a binding binational mechanism for resolving disputes, although Israel was required to sign the GATT subsidies code. Second, it did not really cover services with any binding provisions. Third, it did not fully liberalize Israeli agriculture. Although tariffs were eliminated in principle, non-tariff measures (such as quotas and even outright bans) were permitted in agriculture.[6] Fourth, it did not establish full freedom for investment, although it did deal with trade-related investment issues by ensuring that the export or purchase of domestic goods and services not be a condition for investment or for receiving investment subsidies.

What lessons does the U.S.-Israel agreement provide? In several respects, it could be a noteworthy precedent for a U.S.-Egypt agreement. First, there were strong political motivations for concluding an FTA. Israel, like Egypt, was a key U.S. ally in the Middle East. The agreement helped cement that relationship. Second, Israel had signed a free trade agreement with Europe. That agreement helped rebalance Israel's economic links with the United States and mitigate the trade diversion it entailed. Third, Israel was a relatively minor trading partner for the United States and was already receiving substantial preferential access, so the agreement did not require major economic adjustments. Egypt, as discussed later in the chapter, has a similar relationship. Fourth, Israel faced the potential loss of its preferential access to the U.S. market under the GSP and was able to avoid that loss through the agreement. Similarly, Egypt faces the erosion of its preferential access to the U.S. market as America signs more FTAs. Fifth, the FTA contributed importantly to the broader U.S. trade liberalization strategy by initiating a bilateral free trade track. In this respect, however, the U.S.-Israel agreement is likely to be seen as less interesting today, in view of the move toward greater regional and multilateral liberalization over the past decade.

The Euro-Med Agreements

In the 1970s the European Union signed cooperation agreements with countries from the Mediterranean that provided for duty-free access to EU markets for industrial products and preferential access for agricultural commodities. The agreements were not reciprocal, however, and the countries could apply MFN tariffs to European products.

By contrast, the Euro-Med agreements, launched at the Barcelona Conference in November 1985, aim at achieving reciprocal free trade between the European Union and the Mediterranean countries through the removal of all tariff and nontariff barriers. These agreements are also expected to gradually liberalize agriculture, through preferential reciprocal access; establish conditions for liberalization in services and capital; and encourage the economic integration of the Mediterranean countries through gradual progress toward cumulative rules of origin and toward a harmonization of regulations and norms on standards, conformity certification, metrology and quality control, intellectual property, competition rules, and customs procedures. The agreements also provide financial aid and technical assistance.[7]

Although the agreement with Egypt has not yet been concluded, it will presumably resemble the agreement signed with Tunisia. If so, it will call for the liberalization of Egyptian manufactured imports from the European Union over a twelve-year period (with almost no liberalization in the first five years). Since most Egyptian manufactured products already have duty-free access to the European Union, the major change will be the removal of Egyptian tariffs on EU exports. In cases where Egyptian exports are covered by quotas, these will be liberalized no more rapidly than agreed under GATT.

With respect to several of the other objectives, however, the agreement actually undertakes few concrete and binding measures. Negotiations to improve agricultural access will not be initiated until after January 1, 2000. No specific language is devoted to the right of establishment, that is, FDI. The agreement requires only that "capital flows moving in accordance with current law can move freely," and income can be liquidated and repatriated. The agreement does not guarantee foreign investors the rights of establishment or national treatment. No time frame is established for the liberalization of services, and indeed, no mention is even made of free trade in services as an objective.[8] Antidumping laws continue to apply, although there are commitments to abide by EU competition disciplines in trade-related activities. A key feature of the agreement is economic cooperation and aid. In particular, efforts are to be made to upgrade Egyptian technical and regulatory capacities in addition to providing financial aid.

This agreement, it has been argued, does not go beyond existing multilateral disciplines. It provides little in improved access for agricultural products, requires no liberalization of government procurement, does not ensure free movement of capital, makes no commitment to liberalize services, and retains the antidumping rules.[9]

NAFTA

The unique achievement of NAFTA is that it contemplates virtually complete free trade between two highly developed economies and a developing country within fifteen years.[10] Remarkably for trade between countries at very different development levels, NAFTA will remove all border barriers to trade, including those in hitherto highly protected trade in agriculture and in textiles and automobiles that meet North American content requirements. The agreement is also remarkable in providing no permanent special and differential treatment for Mexico as a developing country.

NAFTA also aims at liberalizing investment and trade in services. It covers all services with obligations for national treatment and rights of establishment unless the service is explicitly excluded. Significantly, the services chapter of the agreement follows a negative-list approach, listing the sectors not covered by the agreement and thereby implying that there will be free trade in all new service areas. Forcing countries to list the sectors in which restrictions remain makes these transparent and indicates where further negotiations should focus. By contrast, a positive-list approach, such as that applied in the GATS agreement, keeps sectors with barriers hidden and protects new sectors unless they are explicitly recognized.

NAFTA institutes a trinational appeals mechanism that can replace existing judicial review by national administrative agencies. It provides a review mechanism to monitor changes in antidumping and countervailing duty laws as applied to partner countries. NAFTA also includes a fairly substantial package on government procurement that goes further than the Canada-U.S. FTA.

Both NAFTA itself and the debate over its ratification demonstrate the advantages and disadvantages of minilateral agreements that go beyond GATT, particularly the problems they pose for countries at different levels of development. For instance, the

U.S.-Canada FTA sparked a heated debate in Canada but was barely noticed in the United States, as was also the case with the U.S.-Israel agreement. By contrast, the NAFTA discussion in the United States has been highly charged. Its opponents argue that NAFTA represents a fundamental threat to U.S. domestic institutions, particularly in the areas of environment and labor standards. Some are concerned about the direct impact of economic development on the Mexican environment in general and its northern border area in particular; others about "leveling down" pressure in the United States, because Mexico offers a safe haven to U.S. firms seeking to evade U.S. regulations on worker safety and environment.

The idea that trade should not occur between countries whose institutions and internal regulatory regimes are "too different" does not fit with the theory of comparative advantage. Nonetheless, it would have probably been impossible to obtain an agreement of the NAFTA type between Canada, the United States, and Mexico without addressing the concerns about the differences in regulatory arrangements.

SIDE AGREEMENTS. On the initiative of the Clinton administration, three accords were signed to go along with NAFTA. They cover the environment, labor issues, and import surges. These accords establish new institutions to monitor conditions, promote compliance, and administer new dispute settlement procedures. These side agreements allow fines to be levied and trade sanctions (suspension of NAFTA benefits) to be applied.

WTO-PLUS? In most respects, NAFTA nations are free to follow domestic policies, but in several areas—such as the administration of trade rules and labor and environmental policies—the enforcement of their own laws is subject to international scrutiny and, sometimes, the threat of trade sanctions. Although no attempt has been made to arrive at a common set of rules and institutional harmonization, steps have been taken, both within the treaty and in parallel to it, to protect intellectual property and mitigate environmental problems linked with trade, and to do so by not relying entirely on voluntary national compliance.

The agreement covering disputes between investors and governments allows complainants to initiate proceedings through either the International Convention for Settlement of Investment Disputes or the United Nations Commission on International Law (UNCITRAL) once all other measures are exhausted. This represents a repudiation by Mexico of the Calvo doctrine, under which countries do not allow foreigners to intervene in disputes over foreign investment.

NAFTA moved considerably beyond the Uruguay Round agreement in liberalizing trade in the areas of foreign investment, services, and intellectual property rights. Under NAFTA investment rules, the restrictions on performance requirements are more extensive than those in the Uruguay Round. The agreement on intellectual property includes products that were under development at the time the agreement was signed. By contrast, these were excluded from Uruguay Round coverage. The agreement on services follows a negative-list approach and extends national treatment coverage to all other sectors, whereas the GATS services agreements applies only to sectors that are listed. The definition of an investment under NAFTA is broader than that under trade-related investment measures, which relates only to goods, or under GATS, which covers only operating services establishments because it includes portfolio investors and commercial real estate.

Two other aspects of NAFTA are particularly noteworthy. First, Mexico took the opportunity of NAFTA to extend the rights granted to U.S. investors to other investors in Mexico. In other words, it liberalized its investment regime multilaterally. Second, NAFTA included textiles and apparel but applied a special, highly restrictive definition of rules of origin in their case, known as the triple transformation rule. That is, the fiber, fabric, and sewing activities must all be performed in North America. Even though the NAFTA countries have not raised their external barriers, this could entail a substantial amount of trade diversion.

UNRESOLVED. Although NAFTA can be classified as a genuine WTO-plus agreement, there are numerous areas in which it goes no further than the WTO. NAFTA does not harmonize competition policies or eliminate administered protection in the areas of antidumping and subsidies.[11] In addition, no specific agreements were signed on the issue of subsidies. In these respects, NAFTA remains a much "shallower" arrangement than the European Union or the Closer Economic Relations Agreement between Australia and New Zealand, in which competition policies replaced administered protection.

Free Trade Area of the Americas

At the Summit of the Americas in Miami in 1994, thirty-four leaders from the Western Hemisphere adopted a U.S. proposal to construct the Free Trade Area of the Americas by the year 2005. In Denver on June 30, 1995, the ministers from these countries agreed to key principles on which to base the FTAA. The trade agreements negotiated through the FTAA will be comprehensive, covering at a minimum the areas explicitly listed in the Summit of the Americas' Plan of Action. Eleven working groups have been established to study market access, customs procedures and rules of origin, investment, standards and technical barriers to trade, sanitary and phytosanitary measures, subsidies, antidumping and countervailing duties, smaller economies, government procurement, intellectual property rights, services, and competition policy. Of course, it remains unclear what the specific nature of these agreements will be, but the United States apparently "plans to use the NAFTA and the WTO as starting points for its objectives in the FTAA negotiations."[12] In other words, this is likely to be a WTO-plus arrangement.

Estimates of the Impact of a U.S.-Egypt FTA

The U.S.-Israel and Euro-Med agreements are examples of free trade agreements that appear to meet the criteria for preferential arrangements contained in Article 24 of GATT, but they do not extend its disciplines. They entail few obligations outside of removing border barriers on industrial products. Although inevitably embellished with language indicating intentions to prepare the way for services liberalization, freer investment, and regulatory reform, in substance they have few binding provisions on these matters. By contrast, an agreement such as NAFTA is of the WTO-plus type. It includes commitments that go further than GATT in agriculture, investment, and services; contains measures to provide oversight of regimes for administered protection; and has side agreements covering labor and environmental standards. To determine which of these options would be a more attractive model for a U.S.-Egypt FTA from an American standpoint, it is essential to consider the major trade barriers in the two economies, the likely effects of such an agreement, and the nature of U.S. interests in such an agreement.[13]

Trade Barriers

Except in the case of textiles and apparel, U.S. tariff barriers to Egyptian exports are low. Indeed, Egypt's preferences under the GSP program and low U.S. tariffs on industrial products generally reduce the average duties Egypt pays on nontextile products to less than 2 percent. There are also few nontariff barriers to agricultural products exported by Egypt to the United States.

As already mentioned, however, barriers are substantial in apparel and textiles. U.S. tariffs in 1992 averaged 8.3 percent on Egyptian textiles and 17.4 percent on clothing, and reached as high as 33–35 percent on clothing products such as sweaters and cotton undershirts. In addition, most Egyptian exports of textiles and apparel to the United States are subject to quotas under the Multifiber Agreement (which covers 87 percent of Egyptian exports of clothing and 34.3 percent of exports of apparel).

Egypt's barriers fall into two broad categories: tariffs and other barriers. In the case of tariffs, these are typically lower than average on most U.S. exports, which are concentrated in noncompeting

agriculture, machinery, transportation, arms, and high-tech products. For many types of capital goods, tariffs are currently 10 percent or less. At the same time, some U.S. products are prevented
from competing in the Egyptian market by the generally high level
of tariffs, which average 16.9 percent on U.S. exports when
weighted by export shares in 1994.[14] Other barriers, as identified
in routine U.S. government reports on foreign markets, include
customs administration and procedures, standards, government
procurement, intellectual property, investment procedures and
rules, competition policy, pharmaceutical price controls, workers' rights, and red tape (see the appendix to this chapter).[15]

Agreement Impacts

In evaluating the effects of a (traditional) free trade agreement
on Egypt and the United States, it is necessary to adjust current
trade data to reflect anticipated changes in trade policy. First, a
sizable share of U.S. imports of textiles and apparel from Egypt
are subject to the Multifiber Agreement scheduled to be fully eliminated by 2005. Second, U.S. and European exports to Egypt are
currently subject to similar tariffs, but by 2010 European products will enter Egypt duty-free. It is therefore reasonable to measure the economic impact of the FTA against a counterfactual in
which U.S. imports from Egypt are somewhat higher and U.S.
exports to Egypt lower than they are at present.

Even with these adjustments, the static economic effects on the
United States are on balance likely to be positive but very small.
Recall that U.S. exports to and imports from Egypt are less than
one-half and one-tenth of 1 percent of total U.S. exports and imports, respectively. Moreover, since they are likely to come into
effect over a decade or more, the impacts on the U.S. economy
will be barely perceptible.

TRADE IMPACT. Outside of the barriers to textiles and apparel,
U.S. barriers to Egyptian products are low. On one hand, the elimination of a low level of tariffs is likely to generate very small in-

creases in imports. On the other hand, the elimination of Egyptian duties averaging 17 percent on a higher level of U.S. exports will generate absolutely larger increases in U.S. exports. This suggests that the overall U.S. bilateral trade balance with Egypt, when compared with what it might have been otherwise, is likely to rise under conditions of bilateral free trade. Some of this increase will occur because of reductions in Egyptian imports from other trading partners both from Europe (as the United States restores parity) and from other trading partners (such as Japan, over which the United States will enjoy preferential access).

In the area of textiles and clothing, the Uruguay Round calls for all quotas on products subject to the Multifiber Agreement to be removed by 2005. Fully half of the changes will occur at the end of the period. This will subject Egyptian exports to two offsetting effects: exports will no longer be constrained by the MFA; but the constraints on other exporters of MFA products to the United States will also be lifted. In addition, if the United States signs other free trade agreements with nations from the Western Hemisphere and elsewhere, Egypt could experience some trade diversion. Although it is not clear which of these effects will dominate, some estimates suggest that Egypt's exports of MFA-constrained products could rise by 54 percent.[16] If, however, the MFA quotas have not been binding on Egypt but have been binding on other suppliers, Egyptian exports could actually be reduced.[17]

By way of example, suppose that removing the quota constraint would raise the value of clothing exports valued at $256 million in 1996 to $394 million.[18] Suppose further that removing the 17.4 percent tariff currently assessed on these products would lower their prices in the United States by 14.8 percent. With an elasticity of 3, this would increase clothing exports by $174 million. A similar calculation for textiles that are subject to lower tariffs suggests an increase of $20 million. All told, therefore, the rise in U.S. imports, scaled by trade in 1996, would be $194 million.[19] (For an overview of Egypt-U.S. trade between 1992 and 1996 by commodity, see table 3-2.)

Other imports from Egypt besides fuel, textiles, and apparel

Table 3-2. *U.S. Trade with Egypt by Commodity, 1992–96*[a]

Millions of dollars

SITC rev 3	Commodity	1992	1993	1994	1995	1996
Exports						
0	Food and live animals	619	564	792	1,131	1,154
1	Beverages and tobacco	27	51	29	52	47
2	Crude materials, inedible, except fuels	158	72	60	163	109
3	Mineral fuels, lubricants, and related materials	49	43	49	70	70
4	Animal and vegetable oils, fats, and waxes	33	22	31	47	44
5	Chemicals and related products, n.e.s.	94	108	87	104	113
6	Manufactured goods classified chiefly by material	115	85	95	133	153
7	Machinery and transport equipment	1,473	1,210	1,030	854	945
8	Miscellaneous manufactured articles	495	580	643	405	484
9	Commodities and transactions not classified elsewhere	24	28	27	28	28
	Total	3,087	2,763	2,844	2,985	3,146
Top 10 commodities						
041	Wheat (including spelt) and meslin, unmilled	450	241	518	760	775
891	Arms and ammunition	398	457	549	317	397
044	Maize (not including sweet corn), unmilled	108	200	167	274	312
792	Aircraft and associated equipment; spacecraft vehicles	747	530	411	145	262
723	Civil engineering and contractors' plant and equipment	79	89	100	138	118
641	Paper and paperboard	43	25	29	48	63

SITC	Commodity					
764	Telecommunications equipment, n.e.s., and parts	193	70	53	68	62
321	Coal, pulverized or not, but not agglomerated	39	39	45	61	55
743	Pumps, air, or other gas compressors and fans	25	39	75	26	49
122	Tobacco, manufacturing whether containing tobacco substitute	26	30	29	35	45

Imports

SITC	Commodity					
0	Food and live animals	6	6	10	8	11
1	Beverages and tobacco	0	0	1	1	1
2	Crude materials, inedible, except fuels	6	5	5	7	14
3	Mineral fuels, lubricants, and related materials	225	362	208	175	229
4	Animal and vegetable oils, fats, and waxes	0	0	0	0	0
5	Chemicals and related products, n.e.s.	2	3	9	9	3
6	Manufactured goods classified chiefly by material	46	50	84	107	83
7	Machinery and transport equipment	2	2	1	2	1
8	Miscellaneous manufactured articles	131	167	213	255	284
9	Commodities and transactions not classified elsewhere in SITC	18	19	17	42	40
	Total	435	613	548	606	665

Top 20 commodities[b]

SITC	Commodity					
333	Crude oil from petroleum or bituminous minerals	176	338	190	159	129
334	Oil (not crude) from petroleum and bituminous minerals	48	24	16	16	100
841	Men's or boys' coats, jackets, textiles, not knit	20	44	69	85	77
842	Women's or girls' coats, capes, textile fabric, not knit	30	43	50	54	69
845	Articles of apparel of textile fabrics, n.e.s.	32	34	36	44	50
931	Special transactions and commodities not classified by kind	16	16	15	40	38

(table continues)

Table 3-2 (continued)

SITC rev 3	Commodity	1992	1993	1994	1995	1996
843	Men's or boys' coats, jackets, textiles, knitted	13	12	13	23	35
651	Textile yarn	16	21	24	33	21
844	Women's or girls' coats, capes, textiles, knitted	15	13	19	24	20
659	Floor coverings	6	6	9	13	20
821	Furniture and parts, bedding, mattresses	3	5	8	9	12
658	Made-up articles of textile materials, n.e.s.	6	6	10	15	11
896	Works of art, collectors' pieces and antiques	14	3	2	6	10
671	Pig iron, spiegeleisen, iron, and steel powder	2	0	2	3	9
676	Iron and steel bars, rods, angles, shapes, and sections	0	0	11	10	7
292	Crude vegetable materials, n.e.s.	4	3	4	4	6
263	Cotton textile fibers	0	0	0	1	6
075	Spices	3	2	5	4	5
652	Cotton fabrics, woven (not narrow or specific fabrics)	15	14	20	24	5
846	Clothing accessories, of textile, knitted or not	3	3	4	5	5

Source: Compiled from official statistics of the U.S. Department of Commerce. Data are unrevised.
a. "0" represents trade of less than $.5 million.
b. Top twenty commodities are sorted by 1996 values.

were valued at $123 million in 1996. Assuming an average reduction in the United States of 2 percent and an elasticity of 2 would lead to an additional increase in imports of $5 million.

In the case of U.S. exports to Egypt, trade here is likely to be depressed as a result of Egypt's Euro-Med agreement and its agreement with the Arab League. It has been estimated that the impact of Egypt's FTAs with Europe and other Arab countries would be to reduce U.S. exports from $2.92 billion to $2.41 billion, when scaled by 1996 values. A traditional FTA with Egypt, however, allows the United States to more than offset this and raises exports to $3.39 billion. This implies that the overall impact of a traditional agreement would be to increase the U.S. trade balance with Egypt by $800 million.[20]

Under a NAFTA-plus agreement that eliminates nontariff barriers, U.S. exports could rise to $4.0 billion, while Egyptian exports to the United States could increase by an additional $75 million. Overall this would increase the U.S. trade balance by $1.3 billion.[21]

Employment Impact

It has become common practice in the United States to estimate the employment impact of such changes. The results are sometimes used to suggest (or imply) that aggregate U.S. employment will increase or decrease by this amount. However, this is not an appropriate approach since it ignores macroeconomic adjustments that will occur in the rest of the economy. The estimates could be used with caution to provide a feel for the adjustment required by shifts in trade flows, although here, again, not all these adjustments would occur in the United States, since a sizable share of U.S. imports from Egypt are likely to replace other U.S. imports rather than domestic production.

In 1994 value added per worker in the United States was $40,600 and $52,700 in apparel and textiles, respectively. If one assumes 6 percent inflation and 6 percent productivity growth between 1994 and 1996, this works out to 23.2 and 17.9 jobs per $1 million, respectively. This implies that the rise in imports from Egypt due to the FTA would have a U.S. employment equivalence of 4,037 jobs in apparel and 357 jobs in textiles, for a total of 4,394 jobs, compared with total U.S. employment in these industries in 1994 of 1.577 million, that is, three-tenths of 1 percent. Using 25 jobs per $1 million (a figure that is typical of labor-intensive industries in the United States such as apparel) would add an additional 125 jobs related to the $5 million worth of other imports. All told, the employment impact on the import side of a traditional FTA would be 4,162.

U.S. exports to Egypt are somewhat less labor-intensive than U.S. imports. Accordingly, the employment content of U.S. exports can be estimated using the average in U.S. manufacturing overall (17 jobs per $1 million of value added). This suggests that an increase in exports of $1.47 million that is associated with a traditional agreement would raise employment related to Egyptian exports by 16,660. Therefore the net employment effects would be a positive 12,498. Again, it should not be assumed that these jobs would be available to unemployed U.S. workers. Many would reflect a shift in the destination of products that might otherwise have been sold in the United States or in other foreign markets. These results are by no means surprising, given that U.S. imports from Egypt are less than a fifth of U.S. exports to Egypt. U.S. exports would be even stronger if the agreement was WTO-plus and covered nontariff barriers. This would add an additional 10,030 jobs, for a total of about 22,500.

In sum, measured in 1996 dollars and scaled by the size of the U.S. and Egyptian economies in that year, a U.S.-Egypt FTA would increase the U.S. bilateral balance with Egypt by about $800 million with a traditional agreement, and by $1.3 billion with a GATT-plus agreement covering NTBs. On balance, net employment related to Egyptian trade would rise by about 12,500 with a traditional agreement, and by 22,500 with a GATT-plus agreement that covered NTBs. The readily quantified impacts on the United States are thus small and unlikely to be the source of much controversy. The major domestic opposition to such an agreement could be expected to come from U.S. textiles and apparel producers.

Terms of the Agreement: Traditional or WTO-Plus?

U.S. interests can be divided into four main categories:

—U.S.-Egypt economic relations. The question of central interest here is whether an agreement would provide economic benefits to the United States by improving resource allocation in a way that will raise U.S. living standards. The immediate concern is how to avoid losing exports represented by the Euro-Med agreement. The United States would also want to improve access to the Egyptian market for U.S. exports and U.S. firms and ensure that U.S. consumers benefit from removing import barriers to U.S. markets, particularly in textiles and clothing.

—Egyptian economic development. The United States is also interested in seeing Egypt develop. Egypt is an important U.S. ally, not simply on questions relating to the peace process between Israel and its neighbors but also in U.S. relations with other countries in the Middle East. Its strategic importance for the United States is evident from the considerable U.S. expenditures on military and economic assistance. Therefore the United States would gain if Egypt was economically prosperous. This would contribute to its political stability and alleviate the need for U.S. aid based on humanitarian concerns.

—Regional economic development. In the view of the United States, an open, dynamic Egyptian economy could play an important role in the Middle East by promoting economic development and peace. Such an economy would provide important markets for other economies in the region and leadership in bringing freer trade and investment to the region.

—U.S. trade policy. The United States has a broader interest in pursuing a trade policy that will lead to a more open global system for trade and investment. As already noted, the United States has adopted a multitrack strategy in which comprehensive free trade and investment agreements play an important role. An agreement with Egypt could contribute to this strategy.

These concerns should be kept in mind when assessing the traditional and WTO-plus options.

A Traditional FTA Agreement

A traditional GATT agreement would in all likelihood counteract the detrimental impact of trade diversion from the Euro-Med agreement on U.S. exports and provide a moderate boost to U.S. exports beyond its current market share. In addition, U.S. consumers would derive some small benefits from reducing barriers to Egyptian exports. Overall, the U.S. trade surplus with Egypt would increase by about $600 million, and net employment related to Egyptian trade would rise by about 9,438. From a U.S. perspective, however, such an agreement would fail to address many of the frustrations U.S. firms have experienced in Egypt with nontariff barriers, administrative practices, and the regulatory environment (see the appendix to this chapter). Its impact on U.S. investment in Egypt would be minimal. U.S. investors, in particular, would be struck by the lack of commitment to liberalizing services, granting rights of establishment, improving access to government procurement, protecting intellectual property rights, and improving the regulatory environment.

A traditional agreement would therefore not make a major contribution to structural reform in Egypt and thus to Egypt's prospects for economic growth. Indeed, the net welfare benefits to Egypt's GNP would be extremely modest.[22] If the U.S.-Egypt Free Trade Agreement is to succeed in fostering Egyptian growth, it will have to help change the general environment for entrepreneurship. It should help make Egypt a more attractive location for both foreign and domestic producers. At the margin, however, a standard GATT agreement would not make a large contribution in these respects, especially in the case of Egyptian producers of manufactured goods outside of textiles, who for the most part already have virtually duty-free access to the United States. All told, therefore, the agreement would be unlikely to provide, directly, a boon to new investment in export industries. Under the agreement, Egyptian markets would not be more contestable by other nations in the region.

The contribution a traditional agreement makes to regional economic integration and development will depend in large part on the rules of origin for textiles and apparel, but it is unlikely to be very great. Since U.S. tariffs are low outside of textiles, the stimulus to regional trade would be small even if cumulation was allowed on value added in other Middle Eastern countries. In textiles, it could be more significant, provided cumulation was allowed. If other regional economies were subject to Egypt's MFN tariffs, however, there could be trade diversion toward U.S. products and away from exporters in the region. This could hurt regional integration.

Concluding such an agreement could also create problems for U.S. trade policy in general. It might suggest that other countries around the world could be given preferential access to the U.S. market without making the kind of commitments to a WTO-plus arrangement represented by NAFTA. In this regard, it would be a retrogression from the thrust of U.S. trade policy in the 1990s. Such an agreement might be seen as establishing a precedent that weakens America's ability to negotiate GATT-plus agreements with other trading partners.

In sum, it might be possible to pass a traditional GATT FTA on the grounds that the United States and Egypt have a unique political and strategic relationship. Such an agreement might also be easier for Egypt to sign since it would not require major adjustments. In underscoring Egypt's reluctance to make more binding commitments in other areas, however, the agreement would actually undermine the credibility of the government's policy pronouncements about liberalization. The image of Egypt being given special and less demanding conditions because of its strategic importance to the United States does little to enhance its economic attractiveness.

A WTO-Plus Agreement

A WTO-plus agreement would be different. As indicated earlier, dealing with nontariff barriers would imply substantially larger quantitative effects. Moreover, the adoption of a more extensive set of commitments patterned after NAFTA, for example, would send a dramatic signal to U.S. and other foreign investors about the changes that have already taken place and that are likely to take place in Egyptian policies.

U.S. firms and products could experience even greater access than estimated above, if Egypt made a broader set of commitments involving national treatment and freedom of establishment for foreign investors, dramatic changes in customs and quality inspections, increased protection of intellectual property, and substantial liberalization of services and government procurement. With a suitable change in the regime, U.S. firms would find investment in Egypt more attractive. They would then be able to employ skilled and unskilled workers in producing goods and services for domestic, regional, and global markets.

A WTO-plus agreement would also strengthen Egypt's ability to engage in domestic reform. If such measures are made part of a binding free trade agreement, they could be more credible than if they were undertaken unilaterally. In addition, if Egypt was open and experiencing rapid growth, the United States would be able to reduce or redirect its aid grants and thereby help Egypt deal with other priorities and play a substantial role in generating growth and prosperity throughout the region.

A key virtue of many of the institutional changes likely to be triggered by a WTO-plus agreement is that by changing administrative practices in Egypt they would facilitate trade and investment with other trading partners both in the region and outside it. If Egypt's customs practices or standards, for example, were streamlined, all who used them would automatically benefit. Similarly, if its intellectual property rules were changed, all outsiders would gain. And if its markets were made more readily contestable, because of regulatory reform, firms from all nations would find it easier to enter and compete. Egypt could readily extend other components of an agreement, such as rights granted to foreign investors, by conferring MFN status on them, as Mexico did under NAFTA.

The more comprehensive the agreement, the fewer the problems for the United States in concluding a preferential agreement and the easier it would be to accept. A WTO-plus agreement with Egypt would represent an extension of U.S. trade policy even further along the multitrack path to freer trade and investment. The specific agreement with Egypt could be one that is readily extended to other countries in the Middle East. A group of countries in the region could even enter into an agreement with the United States plurilaterally, rather than sequentially.

It is important to remember that WTO-plus provisions introduced into NAFTA and the FTAA are not simply a matter of principle. They reflect a coalition of interests that support free trade agreements in the United States and the minimum measures required to placate those who are opposed. In particular, U.S. multinationals hoping to use Egypt as an export platform, to serve both regional markets and the U.S. market, seek assurance that the regime will be hospitable. They need to know that intellectual property will be protected, that national treatment will be safeguarded, and that they will have the right to operate under nondiscriminatory conditions. It may also be necessary for the agreement to include provisions regarding worker and environmental policies, although these are bound to be more controversial.

Conclusions

The United States runs a substantial trade surplus with Egypt that is offset by U.S. expenditures on economic and military assistance. The Egyptian presence in the U.S. market is limited, and aside from petroleum, it is concentrated in exports of textiles and apparel, which are subject to both tariff and quota restrictions. Although U.S. exporters are constrained by many aspects of

Egypt's trade and regulatory environment, the United States has been able to export grains, arms, and specialized equipment fairly successfully. Outside of petroleum, U.S. investment in Egypt is very small.

The U.S. share of the Egyptian market could fall as a result of the Euro-Med and its liberalization to EU products. It could also fall, although by considerably less, in the aftermath of a free trade agreement with the Arab League. Scaled by 1996 exports, these declines together would represent a loss of more than $500 million in U.S. exports to Egypt. Removing U.S.-Egypt tariffs could more than restore this share, boosting exports by $1.5 million and net employment due to Egyptian trade by about 12,500 jobs.

Two distinct models could serve as precedents for a U.S.-Egypt agreement. One model is the traditional GATT FTA, exemplified by the U.S.-Israel and Euro-Med agreements. The U.S.-Israel free trade agreement was the first FTA signed by the United States, and its provisions were somewhat limited. It did not fully liberalize agriculture, contained no binding mechanism to settle international disputes, and did not cover services or foreign investment. It also proved disappointing because of several Israeli nontariff protectionist measures, which continue to create problems. Similarly, the binding provisions of the Euro-Med agreements achieve free trade by concentrating on reciprocal, tariff-free access in industrial products. They achieve only partial liberalization in agriculture, and do not cover services or foreign investment.

The other model, as exemplified by NAFTA, is a WTO-plus arrangement. This model accords more closely with the recent thrust of U.S. trade policies, which have shifted over the postwar period from relying almost exclusively on multilateral negotiations in order to reduce border barriers toward a multitrack strategy that emphasizes domestic policies and barriers to goods, services, and investment. NAFTA includes agriculture on both sides in a meaningful way: it includes services with a negative list and guarantees for direct foreign investors, and it provides for binding resolution of trinational disputes. It also contains side agreements relating to the enforcement of labor standards and measures to protect the environment. Tougher intellectual property rules accompanied the negotiations. The agreements to be negotiated with Chile and other Western Hemisphere countries are likely to have a similar character.

A traditional free trade agreement with Egypt would more than offset the effects of trade diversion on U.S. exports due to the Euro-Med agreements. But it would not really deal adequately with the many barriers faced by U.S. firms in operating in Egypt, nor would it make a major contribution to Egypt's internal reforms and its relationship with other trading partners. By contrast, a WTO-plus FTA with the United States that did eliminate these barriers would boost U.S. employment related to trade by an additional 10,000, facilitate U.S. access, promote Egyptian growth, provide a fulcrum for regional economic growth and trade, and advance America's multitrack approach to freer trade and investment.

Appendix: U.S. Concerns about Egyptian Practices

Several Egyptian practices have been cited as impediments to an FTA with the United States.

Customs Valuation and Procedures

Exporters and importers alike complain that Egypt's method of assessing customs duties is often arbitrary, and that the rates charged are often higher than prescribed in the tariff code. Tariff valuation is based on the so-called Egyptian selling price specified in the commercial invoice that accompanies a product the first time it is imported. Subsequent imports of the same product must have a value not lower than that noted on the invoice of the first shipment. Customs officials routinely increase invoice values from 10 to 30 percent for customs valuation purposes.

Banned Imports

As a result of its commitments in the Uruguay Round, Egypt is phasing out an import ban applied to textiles, apparel, and poultry. The items on the list have had an important impact on American exports of poultry. Recently, Egypt imposed new obstacles to importing previously banned products. Substantial increases in the duty rates of several products such as tractors, cement, and frozen vegetables were imposed immediately after their removal from the ban list in August 1992. The tariff on poultry was increased from 5 to 70 percent. Many items removed from the banned list—including meat, fruits, vegetables, household appliances, construction products, electronic devices, appliances, transformers, and many consumer goods—were added to the list of commodities requiring inspection for quality control before importation.

Standards

Some 1,500 tariff lines (25 percent of the tariff schedule) are subject to quality control. Internationally recommended methods for testing and certification are allegedly ignored, and internationally recognized quality and certification marks may not be accepted. Importers report that testing procedures for imports differ and that tests are carried out with faulty equipment by testers who often make arbitrary judgments. Other product specifications act as barriers to trade. For example, the Ministry of Health requires that beef imported for direct human consumption have less than 7 percent fat, a level virtually never reached in premium beef exports. Sales of $1 million to $2 million of high-quality U.S. beef have allegedly been jeopardized.

Government Procurement

Egypt by law gives national bidders a 15 percent price advantage. The tender process has been criticized for its lack of transparency, poor enforcement of rules, and rigged outcomes. Egypt is not a member of the WTO Government Procurement Agreement.

Intellectual Property

Egypt has increased intellectual property protection over the past few years. The United States has progressively improved its ratings of Egypt's laws and enforcement. Since 1994 Egypt has moved from the priority watch list to the list of countries "to be monitored for progress achieved." Nonetheless, efforts to draft a modern patent law have met with stiff resistance from Egypt's pharmaceutical and chemical industries.

Services

Egypt continues to limit the share of foreign personnel in foreign-controlled enterprises and insists on a maximum of 49 percent of foreign capital in several industries (construction and related engineering services, tourism projects in the Sinai region, insurance). In addition, economic needs tests are required to operate a tourism business or to open branches of foreign banks and insurance (for example, new companies should be able to work without harmful competition to existing companies), and there are restrictions, among others, on the operation of representative offices. It is not difficult to see why Egypt's state-owned telecommunications industry remains heavily regulated.

Investment

In 1991 Egypt removed virtually all categories of direct investment from the negative list requiring prior government approval, with the exception of tobacco, military industries, and Sinai investments. On May 11, 1997, a new investment law reaffirmed basic guarantees for investors and clarified the framework for investment incentives. Under the 1992 U.S.-Egypt Bilateral Investment Treaty (BIT), Egypt is obliged to maintain certain critical elements of an open investment regime. Despite the BIT and further liberalization, securing the approval of foreign investment may entail long procedures and is not yet automatic. The United States has addressed the liberalization of Egyptian investment screening requirements within the R negotiations on TRIMS and in the context of the Gore-Mubarak Partnership for Economic Growth.

Privatization

It is difficult for private firms to compete in sectors dominated by state-owned enterprises. By 1997 Egypt had privatized forty-six firms valued at $3.1 billion. This is a small share of the approximately 300 companies with book values of $27 billion.[23] In 1997 the government was unable to meet its plans for privatizing thirty-three companies.

Competition Policy

Egypt does not have laws prohibiting monopolies, cartels, or conflicts of interest.

Pharmaceuticals

The price control of the pharmaceutical sector has forced U.S. companies to adjust prices to reflect general inflation. U.S. companies occasionally allege discrimination in granting price increases. The concern for foreign pharmaceutical companies is that no more than four similar drugs are allowed in the market, which reduces the ability of companies to expand their product lines.

Workers' Rights

All industrial unions in Egypt are required to belong to the Egyptian Trade Union Federation, the sole legally recognized labor federation. According to the U.S. government, this is in violation of the International Labour Organization's principle of freedom of association.

Red Tape

Major bureaucratic requirements hinder private initiative. Although the government has simplified company registration and streamlined approvals processes, "pervasive red tape remains the number one complaint of both foreign and domestic investors."[24]

Notes

I am grateful to the Institute for Social and Economic Policy in the Middle East (ISEPME) at the Kennedy School of Government, Harvard University, for supporting this research and to Fernando Hernandez-Jimenez for research assistance and participants at a seminar held in Washington, D.C., in October 1997 for their comments.

1. Walker (1997).

2. U.S. Trade Representative (1966), National Trade Estimate Report on Foreign Trade Barriers, p. 10.

3. My research calls these views into question. It suggests the major source of the problems facing workers in the developed countries is changes in technology, in particular, labor-substituting technical change, rather than trade. See Lawrence (1996).

4. For a more complete discussion, see Rosen (1989); Pelzman (1989); and Goldberg, Hirsch, and Sassoon (1988).

5. Until 1995, under Article 10 of the agreement, Israel was allowed for infant industry reasons to increase or reintroduce ad valorem duties not exceeding 20 percent above the agreed level. However, the percentage of products to which this could apply was not to exceed 10 percent of the total value of Israel's imports from the United States. In October 1995 the United States consulted with Israel on bringing the FTAA into compliance with the WTO standard for agriculture liberalization, and Israel has agreed to steady improvements in U.S. access for agricultural goods.

6. Mexico and the United States will have complete free trade within fifteen years, as will Canada and Mexico, except in the areas of poultry, dairy products, and eggs.

7. Hoekman (1995).

8. Hoekman and Djankov (1997b).

9. Hoekman and Djankov (1997b).

10. The obligations on domestic support and export subsidies are merely hortatory. NAFTA actually gives up on the effort to abandon subsidy and countervailing duty rules, which was mandated in the U.S.-Canada FTA.

11. Egyptian tariffs in 1991 were as high as 120 percent. Subsequently there have been several phases of tariff reduction. In February 1995 the government reduced custom duties on eighteen categories of machinery and other durable imported goods from a range of 20–70 percent to a flat rate of 10 percent. In January 1966 there was a similar reduction on twenty-five capital commodities. In October 1996 tariffs were set at 5–55 percent. High rates still apply to automobiles with engines larger than 1,300 cc, alcoholic beverages, and certain luxury items. Furthermore, Egyptian customs assesses a 3 percent or 6 percent service fee on imports, depending on the tariff applied. See U.S. Trade Representative, *Foreign Trade Barriers* (1996, p. 81).

12. U.S. Trade Representative (1996), p. 75.

13. The analysis in this section draws heavily on Hoekman, Konan, and Maskus (this volume, 1998).

14. Calculations are based on data from Hoekman, Konan, and Maskus (this volume, 1998). According to Hoekman and Subramanian (1997), even after full implementation of Uruguay Round commitments in 2005, Egypt's final bound tariffs will remain high, averaging about 62 percent in agriculture, 32 percent in industry, and about 37 percent overall.

15. Among these publications are U.S. Trade Representative reports on foreign trade barriers, commercial guides published by the Department of Commerce, and State Department analyses of current economic trends.

16. Hoekman and Subramanian (1997).

17. Kheir-el-Din and El-Sayed (1997).

18. These assumptions are based on Hoekman and Subramanian (1997).

19. Hoekman, Konan, and Maskus (this volume, 1998) derive smaller estimates, with imports rising by just $56 million in response to traditional FTA.

20. Hoekman, Konan, and Maskus (this volume, 1998), table 8.

21. See Hoekman, Konan, and Maskus (this volume, 1998).

22. See Hoekman, Konan, and Maskus (this volume, 1998).

23. U.S. Department of State, "Economic Trends Report for Egypt," July, p. 3.

24. U.S. Department of State, "Economic Trends Report for Egypt," July, p. 3.

CHAPTER FOUR

Economic Incentives
and Effects

Bernard Hoekman, Denise Konan,
and Keith Maskus

TRADE LIBERALIZATION figures prominently on the policy reform
agenda of the government of Egypt. Tariffs and other barriers to
trade have been reduced significantly since the late 1980s. Egypt
has also participated in multilateral agreements to liberalize the
trade regime: for example, it has bound its tariffs in GATT and
agreed to eliminate quotas on textile imports. Preferential trade
liberalization—under which trade barriers are reduced for only a
subset of trading partners—has always been important in Egypt's
trade policy. In the context of the Arab League, Egypt accords
preferential treatment to imports of Arab countries. Most recently,
agreement was reached in the Arab League to establish a free trade
agreement over a ten-year period starting in 1998.[1] Egypt is also
far advanced in negotiations with the European Union to establish a bilateral FTA, which will lead to the elimination of import
duties and other barriers to trade on goods of EU origin over a
twelve-year period. These developments imply that by 2010 a large
proportion of Egypt's imports will enter the country without en-
countering tariffs.

It has long been thought that the tariff discrimination implied
by an FTA is likely to have two effects.[2] First, members will import some products from firms located in a more expensive partner country, rather than from cheaper suppliers located in

nonmember countries. Second, inefficient domestic production will be replaced with purchases from lower-cost producers located in other member countries. If the first effect (trade diversion) is greater than the second one (trade creation), an FTA might result in lower welfare for a member country. Although the concepts of trade diversion and creation are inadequate measures of the welfare effects of regional integration efforts, the standard policy prescription for reducing the opportunity costs associated with an FTA is to lower average trade barriers on rest-of-the-world imports. Similar incentives arise if large countries negotiate many bilateral FTAs with trading partners. The resulting "hub-and-spoke" nature of the FTAs may give rise to "investment diversion" to the hub country, because firms located in the hub have duty-free access to all "spoke" countries. The potential for investment diversion can only be reduced if all trading partners cooperate and remove barriers on each other's trade. Cooperation is required. The recent Arab League FTA may to some extent have been motivated by a desire to avoid the negative implications of the emerging "hub and spoke" network of bilateral Euro-Med agreements.[3]

Nonmember countries that are "left out" of an FTA will also have an incentive to seek reductions in the external barriers imposed by FTA members. This may be reflected in pressure to engage in multilateral trade negotiations in the context of the World Trade Organization. Alternatively, nonmembers may seek to negotiate an FTA in turn or to accede to the initial FTA. Interest in the negotiation of an FTA between the United States and Egypt is quite likely to be motivated in part by the Euro-Med and Arab League initiatives.

The potential economic implications of a Euro-Mediterranean Partnership Agreement (EMA) for the Egyptian economy has been the subject of a number of analyses in the literature.[4] This chapter explores the economic impact of an Egypt-U.S. FTA, taking the EMA and Arab League agreements as the base case, in order to determine what incentives are created for both Egypt and the United States to conclude an FTA, given the realization of free trade between Egypt and Europe and the Arab League. The discussion begins with a number of conceptual issues and a review of the status quo trade policies that characterize the benchmark for simulation analysis. It then turns to the model, data sets, and the main scenarios that are evaluated, followed by the results of the simulation analyses.

Trade Policy and the Structure of Trade

For purposes of this discussion, bilateral Egyptian trade flows are separated into four regions: the European Union (including Turkey),[5] the United States, the Arab League, and the rest of the world (ROW). The European Union is Egypt's largest trading partner, accounting for roughly 40 percent ($4.5 billion) of merchandise imports in 1995 and absorbing 45 percent ($1.6 billion) of Egypt's exports. The United States comes second in terms of imports, accounting for $2.2 billion in 1995 (19 percent of the total).[6] Although the United States is a significant supplier to Egyptian markets, it absorbs considerably less in exports. In 1995 total exports to the United States were $520 million, much of which comprised textiles and clothing. The Arab League is the second most important export market for Egyptian exports, absorbing $550 million (16 percent of all exports of goods) in 1995. In many product categories—including processed foodstuffs, wood products, paper and printing, glass and mineral products, and transport equipment—more than 50 percent of total Egyptian exports go to Arab markets (table 4-1). In contrast, Egypt imports relatively little from the Arab League region. The most important in terms of import shares are petroleum products, beverages, and textiles and clothing. Despite their large presence in production, vegetable foodstuffs and food processing are major import goods, as are machinery and chemicals. On the export side, Egypt's trade flows are dominated by transport services (largely because of the Suez Canal), oil, tourism, and textiles and clothing.

Two conclusions can be drawn from these statistics. First, al-

Table 4-1. *Benchmark Output and Trade Shares*

Sector	Output	Import				Export			
		Total	European Union	United States	Arab League	Total	European Union	United States	Arab League
Agriculture									
1. Vegetable products, foodstuffs (VG1)	12.4	13.3	11.7	47.9	2.2	2.6	27.0	1.5	63.5
2. Vegetable products, nonfoodstuffs (VG2)	1.7	0.0	36.9	16.5	1.2	0.1	49.3	13.4	14.1
3. Animal products (ANI)	8.0	0.8	82.7	0.0	9.6	0.3	35.2	2.3	53.0
Mining and quarrying									
4. Crude petroleum and natural gas (OIL)	2.7	1.2	52.0	7.0	24.4	18.5	30.6	4.6	1.0
5. Other extractive industries (MIN)	.09	2.0	17.7	14.8	3.5	0.2	56.8	9.2	21.4
Manufacturing									
6. Food processing (FOO)	7.7	15.1	40.3	10.6	2.3	1.3	20.1	4.5	49.3
7. Beverages (BEV)	0.6	0.0	41.7	16.3	28.5	0.0	1.2	0.0	87.6
8. Tobacco products (TOB)	1.9	1.0	27.0	27.4	2.5	0.0	0.4	0.7	45.3
9. Cotton ginning and pressing (TX1)	1.2	0.5	36.9	0.3	0.9	4.2	33.7	0.2	1.4
10. Cotton spinning and weaving (TX2)	5.2	2.4	33.4	7.1	3.7	10.3	72.4	10.9	6.1
11. Clothing: assembled and pieces (CLO)	1.4	0.0	12.4	0.9	19.1	1.2	34.7	49.1	8.6
12. Leather products, excluding shoes (LEA)	0.2	0.0	25.7	0.9	13.8	0.1	48.8	1.5	30.9
13. Shoes (SHO)	0.4	0.0	16.0	2.9	12.0	0.0	20.5	1.9	60.5
14. Wood products, excluding furniture (WOO)	1.1	5.0	39.8	1.4	0.4	0.1	1.5	0.1	86.1
15. Furniture (FUR)	1.4	0.0	57.0	34.7	1.4	0.5	14.9	10.6	58.5
16. Paper and printing (PAP)	1.5	3.3	46.8	17.1	2.9	0.9	1.6	0.8	91.7

17. Chemicals, excluding petroleum (CHE)	3.1	10.8	62.6	12.2	7.9	1.8	31.3	3.5	39.4
18. Petroleum refining (PET)	2.7	1.2	48.4	6.2	28.9	3.3	58.5	0.6	7.2
19. Rubber, plastics, and products (RPL)	0.8	2.3	42.8	20.4	9.8	0.3	41.3	0.7	45.3
20. Porcelain, china, pottery (POR)	0.3	0.4	47.4	7.8	11.5	0.1	42.2	1.5	32.4
21. Glass and products (GLA)	0.3	0.5	63.3	5.3	3.6	0.1	9.3	5.5	62.1
22. Mineral products, n.e.i. (MPD)	1.7	0.4	61.6	3.8	2.2	0.0	4.8	2.0	80.9
23. Iron, steel, other base metals (MET)	2.8	2.6	35.5	11.8	9.0	0.8	68.3	1.9	24.3
24. Machinery and appliances (MAC)	3.5	23.1	59.4	17.4	2.4	4.6	9.5	3.9	58.0
25. Transportation equipment (TRA)	1.0	5.9	33.8	12.1	0.7	0.4	3.6	0.3	89.8
26. Other manufacturing (OMF)	0.1	0.5	47.6	11.2	3.5	0.1	25.4	3.2	62.5
Services and other									
27. Electricity, gas, and water (ELE)	1.7	0.2	44.6	16.8	4.3	0.7	25.0	7.0	40.0
28. Construction (CON)	5.5	0.2	44.6	16.8	4.3	0.8	25.0	7.0	40.0
29. Trade (TRD)	7.1	0.3	44.6	16.8	4.3	5.6	25.0	7.0	40.0
30. Restaurants, hotels, coffeehouses (RES)	2.3	0.0	44.6	16.8	4.3	5.0	25.0	7.0	40.0
31. Transport and storage (TRN)	6.0	1.3	44.6	16.8	4.3	31.9	44.7	6.7	20.2
32. Communications (COM)	0.8	0.1	44.6	16.8	4.3	0.4	25.0	7.0	40.0
33. Financial establishments (FIN)	1.5	1.1	44.6	16.8	4.3	0.0	25.0	7.0	40.0
34. Insurance (INS)	0.3	0.0	44.6	16.8	4.3	0.5	25.0	7.0	40.0
35. Real estate and business services (HSG)	2.8	3.9	44.6	16.8	4.3	0.0	25.0	7.0	40.0
36. Social and community services (SER)	6.0	0.1	44.6	16.8	4.3	0.2	25.0	7.0	40.0
37. Recreational and cultural services (REC)	0.5	0.2	44.6	16.8	4.3	3.2	25.0	7.0	40.0
38. Personal services (PER)	0.9	0.0	44.6	16.8	4.3	0.0	25.0	7.0	40.0

Source: Modified from Maskus and Konan (1997).

though the European Union is by far the largest trading partner of Egypt, trade flows are rather diversified. The non-Arab, non-EU, non-U.S. "rest of the world" provides 34 percent of imports and takes 25 percent of exports. These numbers suggest that the potential for trade diversion from a preferential trade agreement with just one of Egypt's major trading partners is significant. Second, services play an important role in Egypt's current account. In view of the lack of disaggregated data on services trade or its breakdown by region, the modeling exercise that follows it is based on the assumption that the Arab League region has a 40 percent export share, the European Union 25 percent, and the United States 7 percent (see table 4-1). The Arab share is assumed to be higher than for merchandise so as to reflect the similarity in language, the importance of proximity for service delivery, and the prevailing policy of favoring Arab services-related investment.[7]

Although tariffs have been declining in recent years—the maximum tariff was recently reduced to 50 percent—at around 20 to 25 percent the import-weighted average tariff is still relatively high. Tariffs on inputs are often lower than those applied to final goods, with the result that effective rates of protection are often a multiple of nominal rates.[8] All quantitative restrictions have been abolished except on imports on textile products, and the textile bans are scheduled to be eliminated in the coming years as part of Egypt's commitments under the Uruguay Round.[9]

As tariffs and quotas have declined in importance, administrative control of the import process has become more prominent and important. Such controls and "red tape" are reflected in customs clearance procedures, in the enforcement of national health and safety standards, and in the logistics involved in moving shipments to, through, and from ports. These controls impose real trade costs on the private sector, both directly in terms of financial charges and indirectly through the opportunity costs of delays incurred in customs clearance. For example, the General Organization for Export and Import Control (GOEIC) inspects all consignments of goods entering Egypt that are subject to quality control standards. As of 1994 some 1,550 tariff lines, or 25 percent of the tariff schedule, were subject to such controls.[10] As is the case for tariff rates, many of which escalate sharply, fees for goods that are intended for retail sale were generally at least twice as large as those that applied if further processing occurred in Egypt.

Customs clearance practices also increase expected costs for businesses. Practices for valuing goods are problematic. Assessed values are frequently reported to exceed invoice values, and applied tariffs may be a multiple of the statutory rate.[11] Fees charged by the public companies providing port services for handling and storage of goods are much higher than in neighboring countries or nations with which Egypt competes, while these companies do not provide quality service in return. Maritime shipping is also a monopoly of the state-owned Egyptian Maritime Navigation Company, which is reflected in maritime transport costs for shippers, which are 25 percent higher than those confronting competitors in neighboring countries for equivalent routes.

A number of initiatives have been taken in recent years to study and reduce red tape costs. Documentary requirements have been simplified, the incidence of stamp duties reduced, and fees for port and related services lowered. In addition, the shipping monopoly is in the process of being abolished.[12] Although these measures have improved the situation, much more remains to be done. In principle, FTAs could help reduce red tape costs through the simplification and abolition of administrative controls and the harmonization and mutual recognition of standards. If extended to include liberalization of trade and investment in services as well as merchandise trade, input costs for export-oriented producers would fall even further. This analysis explores the relative importance of reducing tariffs, removing red tape costs, and improving the efficiency of the services sectors through improved quality and lower costs.

Model Structure and Benchmark Data

The model used here to analyze the effects of various trade liberalization scenarios is a standard single-country, competitive, computable, general equilibrium model. For many proponents of regional integration, such a model is inappropriate in that it fails to take into account dynamic effects arising from economic integration, due to expanded markets and less uncertainty (because of a "locking-in" or "anchoring" of policy reforms).[13] Dynamic gains may be generated through the realization of economies of scale and competitive gains under imperfectly competitive market structures, as well as through increased investment (including inflows of FDI) in member countries. The rate of economic growth may also increase through higher rates of transfer of technology and greater investment in research and development. The fact is, these claims have so far not been demonstrated conclusively, either theoretically or empirically. The existence of such gains depends heavily on the specific models used and is very sensitive to the characteristics of the member countries, the policies in place before formation of the PTA, and the counterfactual or antimonde being postulated. Given the absence of compelling methodologies to assess the possible dynamic effect of preferential trade liberalization—that is, methodologies firmly grounded in theory and consistent with the empirical evidence—we have chosen to pursue a well-understood, conservative modeling strategy.

It is assumed that Egypt is a price-taker on world markets. Thus policy changes will not be expected to alter prices significantly in other regions of the world.[14] To take into account the impact of the different FTAs noted earlier, Egypt's trade flows are examined across the three major regions of interest (the European Union, United States, Arab League), with all other trade flows collected into a residual "rest of the world." Statutory most-favored-nation tariffs, scaled for consistency with reported tariff revenues, are assumed to apply to imports from each of these regions in the benchmark case. These tariffs are weighted across subsectors by global import shares. To take into account existing preferential trade within the Arab region, applied tariffs on intra-Arab trade are set at 40 percent of the MFN levels.[15]

In keeping with standard practice in the literature, final outputs are produced according to a Leontief function using intermediate inputs and real value added. A constant elasticity of substitution (CES) production function describes the substitutability between labor and capital inputs in producing real value added. Intermediate inputs and final goods are differentiated by country of origin according to the Armington assumption, so that export and import prices differ across regions.[16] In each sector, demand for domestically produced and imported goods is represented by a CES function, and intermediate imports are also differentiated by region of supply in a CES structure. Similarly, Egyptian industries supply regionally differentiated goods to both domestic and foreign markets (exports). Production follows a nested two-stage constant elasticity of transformation (CET) function. Total output is first calculated as the sum of domestic supply and total exports, with the latter then being allocated across regions (the European Union, United States, Arab League, and rest of the world) according to a sub-CET function.

A representative consumer maximizes a nested CES utility function with a corresponding multistaged budget constraint. She receives income from primary factors (labor and capital), net transfers from the government, the current-account deficit, as well as any net economic rents from the operation of nontariff barriers to trade. The cost-of-living index associated with the utility function is chosen as numeraire. Changes in aggregate consumption are a direct measure of welfare impacts ("equivalent variation"). Capital is assumed to be partly mobile in the sense that there are a number of resource-constrained sectors, which we take to be agriculture (VG1, VG2, ANI), mining (OIL, MIN), utilities (ELE), and transport (TRN). In all other sectors capital is freely mobile. The intention underlying this assumption is to capture the strong possibility in Egypt of resource constraints that limit intersectoral factor flows and output changes. In particular, Egyptian experts seem concerned about their country's ability to expand agricultural production in the face of significant water scarcities. There are also constraints on output in crude petroleum and the Suez Canal, the latter of which justify including the transport sector.

Intermediate inputs are disaggregated into domestic sources

and imports to incorporate importing costs and tariffs in purchases for the production sector. Sector-specific proportionate import costs and export costs capture the impact of administrative NTBs, or "red tape." As already mentioned, significant NTBs in Egypt include licensing fees, inspection delays, monopoly port charges, difficulties due to inadequate transport facilities, excessive and arbitrary enforcement of product standards, and restrictive licensing schemes and qualification requirements for professional service providers. These NTBs drive wedges between home and foreign prices. Conservatively, it is assumed that there are no resource-using rent-seeking costs in the economy, so that NTB "taxes" represent a pure transfer among domestic agents. The "revenues" are allocated to the representative agent, so that a reduction in import NTBs simply increases the consumer's purchasing power.[17]

Any FTA will have a direct impact on government finances in Egypt since import duties constitute more than 15 percent of tax revenues and more than 10 percent of total current revenues (including transfers from public firms). Account is therefore taken of the fiscal consequences of tariff reform.[18] In this connection it is assumed that the government operates under a fixed deficit constraint, so changes in tariff collections are compensated by an endogenous domestic tax change to ensure that liberalization is revenue-neutral. Required changes in domestic tax collections are achieved by varying the goods and service tax (GST), a sales tax that applies to final consumption and capital investment of domestic goods and imports but does not apply to exports.[19] As shown in table 4-2, the GST is applied on sales of goods and services at rates ranging from 0 to 25 percent; the standard rate is 10 percent.[20]

Two standard closure rules are imposed: the savings-investment balance and a fixed current account balance. The first is based on the assumption that the capital stock is exogenously fixed at the benchmark level and is financed through forced consumer savings that act as a direct (lump-sum) tax. A capital good is modeled as composite goods of fixed composition. Firms buy

Table 4-2. *Government Policy and Elasticity Parameters*
Percent

Sector	GST 1994 (percent)[a]	Egypt's tariff, 1994	Arab MFN tariffs (import-weighted)[b]	Capital-labor elasticity of sub-stitution
Agriculture				
1. Vegetable products, foodstuffs (VG1)	0.0	2.5	6.3	0.95
2. Vegetable products, nonfood-stuffs (VG2)	10.0	6.7	28.9	0.95
3. Animal products (ANI)	0.0	4.4	6.7	0.95
Mining and quarrying				
4. Crude petroleum and natural gas (OIL)	0.0	8.2	2.9	0.43
5. Other extractive industries (MIN)	10.0	7.0	15.6	0.43
Manufacturing				
6. Food processing (FOO)	0.0	6.8	18.3	0.95
7. Beverages (BEV)	10.0	953.2	14.8	0.95
8. Tobacco products (TOB)	10.0	65.5	83.1	0.95
9. Cotton ginning and pressing (TX1)	10.0	17.3	24.9	0.93
10. Cotton spinning and weaving (TX2)	10.0	23.3	17.4	0.93
11. Clothing: assembled and pieces (CLO)	10.0	53.7	32.5	1.19
12. Leather products, excluding furniture (LEA)	10.0	34.8	44.6	0.75
13. Shoes (SHO)	10.0	51.8	36.9	0.75
14. Wood products, excluding furniture (WOO)	5.0	8.1	28.1	0.93
15. Furniture (FUR)	10.0	46.9	34.9	0.93
16. Paper and printing (PAP)	0.0	13.3	18.6	1.00
17. Chemicals, excluding petroleum (CHE)	5.0	8.9	17.6	1.01
18. Petroleum refining (PET)	0.0	7.1	20.0	0.43

(table continues)

Table 4-2 *(continued)*

Sector	GST 1994 (percent)[a]	Egypt's tariff, 1994	Arab MFN tariffs (import-weighted)[b]	Capital-labor elasticity of sub-stitution
19. Rubber, plastics, and products (RPL)	10.0	15.6	24.7	0.97
20. Porcelain, china, pottery (POR)	10.0	43.5	21.3	0.93
21. Glass and products (GLA)	10.0	29.6	17.2	0.97
22. Mineral products, n.e.i. (MPD)	5.0	18.1	12.7	0.43
23. Iron, steel, other base metals (MET)	10.0	17.2	32.6	0.43
24. Machinery and appliances (MAC)	25.0	17.9	19.9	1.20
25. Transportation equipment (TRA)	25.0	41.2	56.6	1.88
26. Other manufacturing (OMF)	10.0	19.3	24.9	1.19
Services and other				
27. Electricity, gas, and water (ELE)	2.5	0.0	0.0	1.88
28. Construction (CON)	10.0	0.0	0.0	1.99
29. Trade (TRD)	8.0	0.0	0.0	1.28
30. Restaurants, hotels, coffee-houses (RES)	8.0	0.0	0.0	1.99
31. Transport and storage (TRN)	0.0	0.0	0.0	1.88
32. Communications (COM)	5.0	0.0	0.0	1.99
33. Financial establishments (FIN)	8.0	0.0	0.0	1.99
34. Insurance (INS)	0.0	0.0	0.0	1.99
35. Real estate and business services (HSG)	8.0	0.0	0.0	1.99
36. Social and community services (SER)	10.0	0.0	0.0	1.99
37. Recreational and cultural services (REC)	8.0	0.0	0.0	1.99
38. Personal services (PER)	10.0	0.0	0.0	1.99

Source: Based on Maskus and Konan (1997) and authors' calculations.
a. Adjusted to be consistent with the real value of the 1990 government deficit.
b. In simulations it is assumed that applied rates are 60 percent of these MFN rates.

composite capital according to their preferences. The interest rate (an index price of the composite capital stock) is endogenous and determined by factor demand.[21] Foreign currencies are scaled so that the appropriate GDP deflator ("world" price index) is unity. The current account can be kept fixed while international prices are constant by means of a change in the home "real exchange rate," which refers implicitly to a change in the home price index (generated by changes in price of home-produced goods) sufficient to sustain a constant current-account deficit measured at world prices.[22] Because the current account is in deficit, it represents an addition to the representative agent's income through exogenous capital inflows.

The data for the model consist of a social accounting matrix (SAM) and other parameters, such as elasticities of substitution and transformation,[23] import and export trade flows by region, and tax and tariff rates. These data are assembled into a consistent set of relationships between intermediate demand, final demand, and value-added transactions using the 1989/90 input-output table for Egypt, updated to incorporate trade and tax policies and trade shares as of 1994.[24] Trade and tariff data by eight-digit HS line were aggregated to the input-output sectoral basis using import weights consistent with the concordance between the input-output table and the tariff classification. From these data, regional trade shares for 1994 were applied to 1990 trade volumes on the input-output basis.[25] Because Egypt does not realize the full revenue that would obtain if statutory tariff rates were applied to all imports because of various exemptions for duty-drawback provisions and investment incentives, weighted legal tariff rates were scaled downward (by some 20 percent) to ensure consistency with total import duty collections in 1994.

To take into account the existence of the quantitative restrictions on imports of textiles and clothing, the statutory MFN rates for this sector have been doubled. It is assumed further that the cost impacts of "red tape" on merchandise imports and exports are 10 and 5 percent, respectively. Egyptian import and export NTBs with Arab countries are assumed to be half those facing other trading partners (5 and 2.5 percent, respectively, on imports and exports of goods), so as to reflect past integration efforts within the region. In the absence of reliable quantitative measures of the price impacts on restrictions on services trade, a uniform 15 percent tax equivalent is imposed on prices of both exported and imported services.[26] Here again it is assumed that there is less discrimination against Arab service suppliers, reflected in a lower 7.5 percent wedge.

Preferential Trade Liberalization: Simulations and Results

Three preferential trade-liberalization scenarios for Egypt are analyzed with the model. Two are "shallow integration" FTAs. The first of these assumes that Egypt implements a partnership agreement with the European Union as well as the Arab League FTA. Under the former, Egypt removes all tariffs on EU goods, and the European Union responds by providing somewhat improved access to its markets.[27] This access is assumed to be equivalent to a 1 percent increase in export prices to the European Union for all commodities except agricultural goods and clothing, where a 2 percent terms of trade improvement occurs (VG1, VG2, ANI, TX1, TX2, CLO). We posit these limited impacts because Egypt already enjoys duty-free access to EU markets for manufactures and is not likely to obtain significantly better market access for agricultural produce.[28]

The Arab League FTA is a standard preferential trade agreement that eliminates tariffs on intra-Arab trade in merchandise. As mentioned previously, little is known regarding the tariffs effectively applied on intra-Arab trade flows. Because the Arab region is a major destination of Egyptian exports and its tariff levels are significantly higher than those applied in the EU and U.S. markets, liberalization of Arab trade barriers could have a major impact on Egyptian welfare. In our scenarios it is assumed that applied Arab tariffs on intra-Arab trade are 60 percent of the statutory MFN rates.[29]

Although only the Arab League agreement has been formally incorporated into Egyptian law (the Euro-Med is still under negotiation at the time of writing), we consider their joint implementation an appropriate base case because they presumably will be an important factor motivating discussions on an FTA with the United States. A potentially important aspect of any FTA is an associated reduction of administrative and other nontariff barriers to Egyptian trade. Although the draft EMA devotes considerable attention to these issues insofar as it deals with technical and financial assistance to ensure greater harmonization and upgrading of customs, standards-related institutions, and infrastructure, it contains no explicit commitments on the part of Egypt to undertake action in these areas. Nor does the agreement commit Egypt to any actions to liberalize access to its service markets or to grant a general right of establishment for foreign investors. We therefore assume that the EMA and Arab League agreements will do nothing to remove the various NTBs discussed earlier.

The second scenario adds a shallow Egypt-U.S. FTA to this mix. In this case, Egypt would eliminate all tariffs on imports from the United States, and the United States would grant Egypt duty-free and quota-free access to its markets. Given that U.S. trade policy toward Egypt is already quite liberal, Egypt again has little to gain in terms of improved access to the United States. We assume therefore that Egypt's export prices in U.S. markets increase by only 1 percent. However, for agricultural products and clothing, which currently do not have free access to those markets, we assume that export prices increase by 8 percent.

The third scenario shows the possible effects of implementing a WTO-plus agreement with the United States. It goes beyond the "shallow" FTA scenarios by eliminating not only tariffs but also all the NTBs applying to both goods and service sectors in Egypt. The motivation for this assumption is that a WTO-plus agreement must extend to investment and trade in services: no "opting-out" would be allowed in these areas, in contrast to the

EMA and Arab League agreements. It is assumed further that the elimination of NTBs is applied on a nondiscriminatory basis. That is, all traders benefit from the associated cost reductions.[30]

Two final scenarios suggest the implications of nondiscriminatory, unilateral elimination of all tariffs and NTBs. The first assumes that Egypt does this on its own. As a result, it does not benefit from preferential access to EU, U.S., and Arab markets but also is not subjected to the trade diversion costs that are associated with FTAs. The second assumes that Egypt unilaterally liberalizes its trade regime on a nondiscriminatory basis, and that this is also pursued by the European Union, the Arab League, and the United States. Given the fact that the EMA and Arab League FTAs should be implemented by 2010, this is a more realistic appraisal of nondiscriminatory liberalization by Egypt. The various scenarios may be summarized as follows:[31]

—*Shallow EMA and Arab League FTAs.* Egypt eliminates all tariffs with the European Union and Arab League (except beverages and tobacco). The European Union grants improved market access, increasing agriculture and textile prices by 2 percent and all other goods by 1 percent, and Arab League countries eliminate their tariffs (except BEV and TOB) with Egypt.

—*Shallow EMA, Arab, and U.S. FTAs.* Same as preceding arrangement except that Egypt eliminates tariffs with the United States. The United States grants improved market access in agriculture and clothing, with export prices rising by 8 percent. All other export prices increase by 1 percent.

—*EMA-Arab FTAs with a WTO-plus with the United States.* Combines first scenario with a deep integration agreement with the United States. The latter results in the removal of all NTBs on a nondiscriminatory basis.

—*Unilateral liberalization.* Egypt unilaterally eliminates all tariffs and all NTBs on an MFN basis. No preferential market access in the United States, European Union, or Arab League.

—*Concerted unilateral liberalization.* Egypt unilaterally eliminates all tariffs and all NTBs on an MFN basis. The United States, European Union, and Arab League grant duty-free access to Egypt.

Table 4-3. *Shallow Integration: Welfare and Fiscal Impact of a U.S.-Egypt FTA*

Impact	EMA-Arab FTAs	EMA, Arab, and U.S. FTAs
Change in welfare (percent)	0.99	1.26
Change in GST (percent)	–2.88	5.26
Average tariff (percent)	4.11	2.65
Trade creation (millions of dollars)	252	342
Trade diversion (millions of dollars)	233	197

Table 4-3 reports results for the first two shallow integration scenarios. The joint EMA and Arab League FTAs generate an estimated welfare gain of 1 percent over benchmark 1994 levels.[32] The trade-weighted average tariff rate falls to 4.1 percent. At $252 million, estimated trade creation gains are only slightly higher than trade diversion losses ($233 million).[33] Trade creation is defined as the sum of import trade creation (consumer surplus net of tariff losses) plus export trade creation (change in producer surplus on trade with the partners).[34] Trade diversion comprises the loss of tariff revenues on imports from non-FTA members resulting from a substitution to partner imports.

A particularly striking result is that the GST can be lowered slightly following the implementation of the FTAs. This arises because of a rise in domestic tax collection as economic activity increases in sectors that are relatively heavily taxed. Thus, despite a significant decrease in tariff collections following implementation of the FTAs, government budget neutrality implies a reduction in the GST. This reflects the fact that the tariff elimination induces resources and consumption to move into sectors that are subject to relatively high GST rates (as well as other taxes). Of course, this will only occur if GST revenues are actually collected. It should also be kept in mind that this result obtains once the adjustment to the new set of incentives has been completed and resources have been reallocated across sectors. During the transition to the new equilibrium the government will most likely experience a decline in revenues.[35]

A shallow FTA between the United States and Egypt that is limited to the abolition of tariffs would be beneficial to Egypt in that welfare would rise in relation to the EMA-Arab FTAs by some 25 percent, to 1.26 percent of GDP (table 4-3, last column). In part this is due to the elimination of some of the trade diversion that would otherwise occur: trade creation now becomes significantly larger than trade diversion. With the extension of duty-free treatment to imports from the United States, the import-weighted average tariff rate falls to only 2.6 percent. It now becomes necessary to increase the GST by about 5 percent in order to maintain budget neutrality. The positive impact on welfare suggests that Egypt has an incentive to negotiate an FTA with the United States.

The incentives for the United States can be detected from the impact of the Arab and EMA agreements on U.S. exports to Egypt.[36] These two FTAs will reduce imports from the United States by $412 million, or 14 percent in relation to the benchmark (table 4-4). The U.S. share of the Egyptian import market falls from 18 to 14 percent. Since these numbers are not very large, U.S. industries may not be too concerned about the trade diversion associated with the Arab and EU FTAs. However, the value of EU exports to Egypt increases by 38 percent or $2 billion under the Arab-EU FTA scenario. U.S. exporters may therefore perceive their opportunity costs to be higher than the "pure" trade diversion if they believe that over time total trade will expand, leaving them with a smaller share of the growing pie.

In percentage terms, the greatest changes in trade flows occur in the FTA with the Arab League. Total imports from Arab countries rise by 33 percent, while exports to the Arab League increase by 44 percent. Given that Egypt traditionally exports much more to the Arab region than it imports, the Arab League's share of total Egyptian exports rises to 40 percent (up from 31 percent). This large increase stems from the fact that market access for Egyptian exports resulting from the two FTAs shows the greatest improvement in the Arab markets. Tariffs within the Middle East

Table 4-4. *Shallow Integration: Impact on Trade Flows*

Trade flow	EMA-Arab FTA	EMA-Arab-U.S. FTA
Percentage share		
EU in total exports	31.0	30.5
EU in total imports	54.7	50.5
U.S. in total exports	4.2	5.2
U.S. in total imports	14.1	20.1
Arab League in total exports	40.3	40.2
Arab League in total imports	5.0	4.7
Millions of dollars		
Exports to EU	49	43
Imports from EU	1,990	1,530
Exports to U.S.	−16	40
Imports from U.S.	−412	629
Exports to Arab League	586	600
Imports from Arab League	170	138
Percentage growth		
Exports to EU	3.2	2.8
Imports from EU	38.2	29.3
Exports to U.S.	−7.0	17.5
Imports from U.S.	−14.3	21.9
Exports to Arab League	44.4	45.8
Imports from Arab League	33.3	26.7

are significant, even if the assumed 40 percent preference margin is taken into account. Trade with the European Union is already duty-free, so that the effect of an EMA in this regard is much smaller. The assumed exogenous rise in export prices in the European Union is nonetheless quite important. Without this assumption, Egypt's exports to the European Union fall by 2.5 percent (not reported) rather than rise by 2.8 percent, as reported in table 4-3. The rise in welfare also becomes significantly less, falling to 0.81 percent (not reported).

One might question the magnitude of the increase in exports to the Arab League, given that these are not large markets. However, it is often noted that intraregional trade between Arab League countries is well below its potential, especially if the Persian Gulf states are excluded. Intraregional trade represents less than 3 percent of the total trade of Middle East and North African countries. Given the potential for further specialization and intra-industry trade, intraregional trade should be able to grow substantially.[37]

If a shallow FTA with the United States were to be added to the other two FTAs, total Egyptian imports from the United States would rise by $629 million (or 22 percent) in relation to the benchmark but would incur a loss of $412 million otherwise (table 4-4). This difference of some $1 billion is a better measure of the incentive for U.S. exporters to support an FTA with Egypt insofar as it includes what might be gained beyond offsetting the threatened trade diversion. In aggregate terms, much of the export gains accruing to U.S. exporters are offset by a decline in the growth of EU exports to Egypt. The rest of the world, not surprisingly, is likely to be a loser from the various FTA combinations. Under the EMA and Arab League FTAs, the ROW share of total imports falls by 25 percent; and it drops by 30 percent if these are complemented by a shallow FTA with the United States (not reported).

It is unlikely that an FTA with the United States would be limited to a shallow agreement of the type that has been reached with the European Union and the Arab League.[38] Instead, the United States can be expected to insist on an agreement that includes liberalization of investment (national treatment, right of establishment, binding arbitration), service markets, and government procurement, as well as disciplines to ensure that domestic legislation and regulations are applied correctly and transparently. Such a WTO-plus agreement would imply that over time the service sector inefficiencies would be removed, and that the prevalence of import- and export-related NTBs would be attenuated. In our simulation, the effects of such an agreement lead to the complete elimination of all NTBs on goods and services.[39] Moreover, this elimination benefits all trade, not just that with the United States, by virtue of affecting domestic regulatory procedures that tend to be applied identically to all traders and investors.

Table 4-5. *Deep Integration: Impact of a WTO-Plus Agreement*

Impact	EMA-Arab FTA with a WTO-plus	Unilateral liberalization of tariffs and NTBs	EMA-Arab FTA with unilateral liberalization of tariffs and NTBs
Change in welfare (percent)	1.84	1.51	2.31
Change in indirect taxes (percent)	6.1	26.0	22.8
Average tariff (percent)	2.6	0	0
Trade creation (millions of dollars)	450	. . .	. . .
Trade diversion (millions of dollars)	170	. . .	. . .

A WTO-plus accord would be significantly more beneficial to Egypt than the shallow FTAs (table 4-5). The positive welfare impact of eliminating NTBs as well as tariffs rises to 1.8 percent of GDP (an increase of almost 50 percent in relation to the EMA and Arab FTAs). Trade creation is almost three times larger than trade diversion, and the absolute magnitude of diversion is lower than under the shallow FTA options. This suggests that the ROW may be somewhat less damaged as well. The underlying trade volumes also increase significantly (not reported). Total imports rise by 25 percent in volume terms, while exports increase by more than 30 percent. As reported in table 4-6, U.S. exports to Egypt rise by $1.1 billion in relation to the 1996 base. This suggests that the total "opportunity cost" of not pushing for a WTO-plus agreement, given the implementation of the European Union and Arab League agreements, is some $1.5 billion (1.1 billion plus 400 million). Also noteworthy in the WTO-plus case are the significant increases in exports to the European Union and the United States, as Egyptian industries benefit from the reduction in real costs associated with producing for export. Exports to the European Union

Table 4-6. *Deep Integration: Impact on Trade Flows*

Trade flow	EMA-Arab FTA with a WTO-plus	Unilateral liberalization of tariffs and NTBs	EMA-Arab FTA with concerted unilateral liberalization of tariffs and NTBs
Percentage share			
EU in total exports	34.2	37.0	34.0
EU in total imports	50.8	43.1	43.0
U.S. in total exports	5.9	5.7	4.6
U.S. in total imports	20.2	17.7	17.7
Arab League in total exports	34.1	26.5	35.9
Arab League in total imports	4.3	3.7	3.7
Millions of dollars			
Exports to EU	478	628	540
Imports from EU	2,467	1,315	1,490
Exports to U.S.	115	105	52
Imports from U.S.	1,119	627	717
Exports to Arab League	546	123	720
Imports from Arab League	150	70	83
Percentage growth			
Exports to EU	31.8	41.8	36.0
Imports from EU	47.3	25.3	28.6
Exports to U.S.	51.3	46.5	22.9
Imports from U.S.	38.8	21.7	25.0
Exports to Arab League	41.4	9.4	54.5
Imports from Arab League	29.4	13.7	16.2

rise by one-third, while those to the United States increase by more than 50 percent. The total value of exports rises by more than 40 percent, as compared with only 15 percent under a set of shallow FTAs (not reported).

For comparison purposes, tables 4-5 and 4-6 also report the results of simulating the economic effects of two unilateral liberalization programs. It is well known that preferential trade liberalization is an exercise in the second best: as long as barriers to foreign competition can be removed on a nondiscriminatory (MFN) basis, associated welfare gains will be higher than if they are limited to only a subset of trading partners. This is confirmed by the simulations. Welfare under MFN liberalization (tariffs and NTBs) rises by 25 percent in relation to what would obtain under a WTO-plus agreement, as long as it is assumed that the Arab League, the European Union, and the United States also liberalize access to their markets. This is not the case if the Arab League maintains trade barriers against Egypt (second column of table 4-5), in which case the predicted increases in exports to Arab countries are also much smaller (table 4-6). A WTO-plus also generates significant trade diversion (table 4-6). Increases in imports from the United States, European Union, and Arab countries are about $1.7 billion less under a unilateral liberalization scenario that is not associated with a reduction in Arab League trade barriers. As total trade increases by roughly the same order of magnitude under both the WTO-plus and unilateral liberalization options, this is trade that is diverted from the rest of the world.

From a political economy perspective, it is useful to know which specific group of U.S. exporters would be most negatively affected by the EMA-Arab FTAs, and which would most benefit from a WTO-plus agreement between Egypt and the United States. According to the various simulations, most of the increase in Egyptian imports to emerge from the FTAs will likely be concentrated in labor-intensive light manufacturing, especially textiles and clothing, leather, footwear, and furniture (table 4-7). These are not sectors in which the United States has a comparative advantage. Instead, U.S. exports to Egypt are concentrated in agricultural produce, machinery and equipment, and pharmaceuticals. Under the shallow-integration FTAs, little change is expected in imports of products where the United States has a revealed comparative advantage in the Egyptian market. Under a WTO-plus, however, imports of most products increase 20–50 percent, even in services, which do not witness much import expansion under the shallow FTAs.

The sectoral implications for the United States of not reacting

Table 4-7. Changes in Imports by Sector

	Change in total import volume (percent)		
Import	Shallow EMA + Arab FTA	Shallow EMA, Arab, and U.S. FTAs	EMA, Arab FTA and WTO-plus
Edible vegetable	1.0	3.1	15.9
Nonedible vegetable	5.3	8.4	50.1
Animal products	8.8	9.3	28.7
Crude oil, gas	8.3	9.3	41.1
Other mining	−.02	−0.3	11.0
Food processing	6.7	8.1	22.4
Beverages	0.3	−0.3	8.9
Tobacco	87.1	120.1	162.1
Cotton yarns, fabric	55.8	61.8	93.6
Clothing	204.7	203.6	258.5
Leather	44.3	44.3	69.3
Footwear	61.6	64.7	94.2
Wood products	5.0	4.9	10.7
Furniture	82.4	105.2	144.9
Paper, printing	8.4	10.1	19.8
Chemicals	7.3	7.9	18.4
Oil refining	11.5	12.2	29.2
Rubber, plastics	12.8	15.8	28.6
Ceramics	57.6	60.0	79.9
Glass	36.4	37.5	56.9
Mineral products, n.i.e.	27.4	28.0	52.4
Iron, steel	18.0	29.9	36.0
Machinery	10.2	11.1	18.9
Transport equipment	24.4	26.7	37.0
Other manufacturing	16.0	18.4	35.0
Electricity, gas, water	1.0	1.1	47.7
Construction	−1.0	−1.6	41.3
Distribution	3.9	3.9	54.2
Hotels, restaurants	1.7	1.3	43.8
Transport	0.6	0.7	44.4
Communications	2.9	2.9	52.6
Finance	2.8	2.8	42.2
Business services	2.8	2.8	40.1
Recreation	−0.4	−0.5	46.5

to the EMA and Arab agreements and the "opportunity costs" of not concluding a WTO-plus agreement to complement these FTAs are reported in table 4-8. Although the primary U.S. export sector—agricultural produce—is not very sensitive to the FTAs, other important export items such as paper, chemicals, machinery, and transport equipment are significantly affected. The EMA-Arab FTAs would cause U.S. machinery exports to fall by 37 percent, while transport equipment and textile fabric exports would drop by almost 50 percent. If the United States concluded a WTO-plus, however, exports of fabrics would rise by a factor of four, transport equipment exports would double, while machinery exports would expand by 35 percent. Other sectors in which exports expand significantly include foodstuffs and rubber and plastics (up 45 percent) and iron and steel (up 80 percent). If trade levels simulated under the EMA-Arab FTA scenario are used instead of the basic calibration as the benchmark for comparison, the associated increase in U.S. exports is even higher. Exports of transportation equipment increase by a factor of four or more and cotton fabrics by a factor of seven, while exports in sectors such as machinery, iron and steel, rubber and plastics, and paper double. Note also that as a result of the liberalization of access to service markets under a WTO-plus agreement, U.S. exports of financial and business services are expected to increase substantially, rising by some 40 percent.

Conclusions

The EMA and Arab FTAs have positive welfare implications for Egypt. However, the gains are much smaller than what could be achieved if these agreements were used to eliminate not just tariffs but real NTB-related trade costs as well. It appears that neither of these two agreements will do much to achieve a significant reduction in NTBs in the short to medium run, although the EMA has the potential to do so. An Egypt-U.S. FTA is likely to be similar to the WTO, and the United States may well seek to con-

Table 4-8. *Imports from the U.S. by Sector under Alternative FTAs*
Millions of U.S. dollars

Sector	"1996 base"[a]	Shallow EMA-Arab FTA	Shallow EMA, Arab, U.S. FTA	EMA, Arab FTAs, and WTO-plus
Agricultural goods	1,150	1,140	1,240	1,300
Crude oil, gas	14	12	16	21
Other mining	47	44	57	65
Food processing	211	188	267	306
Beverages	0	0	0	0
Tobacco	9	4	32	38
Cotton yarns, fabric	15	8	47	58
Clothing	0	0	1	2
Leather	0	0	1	2
Footwear	0	0	0	0
Wood products	8	7	10	11
Furniture	0	0	1	1
Paper, printing	76	59	100	109
Chemicals	165	131	189	210
Oil refining	8	7	9	11
Rubber, plastics	55	41	73	83
Ceramics	3	1	6	7
Glass	3	2	5	6
Mineral products, n.i.e.	2	1	3	3
Iron, steel	37	29	58	67
Machinery	665	420	830	890
Transport equipment	280	140	356	540
Other manufacturing	5	3	8	9
Electricity, gas, water	4	4	4	6
Construction	5	5	5	7
Distribution	9	9	9	14
Hotels, restaurants	0	0	0	0
Transport	29	29	29	42
Communications	2	2	2	3
Finance	30	31	31	44
Business services	85	87	87	121
Recreation	5	5	5	7
Total	2,920	2,410	3,390	3,980

Source: Authors' calculations.

a. Imports are valued at original base-year domestic prices, were converted to U.S. dollars, and adjusted to take into account the growth in Egypt's total imports between 1990 and 1996. U.S. exports of arms and ammunition are excluded (equal to some $400 million in 1996).

clude an agreement that goes further than the WTO. Such an agreement would consequently not only help to reduce the trade diversion costs for the United States that are associated with the EMA and Arab League FTAs, but, what is more important from an economic perspective, it would generate a significant increase in Egypt's welfare by helping to reduce the prevalence of nontariff barriers and "red tape" costs. The modeling exercise suggests that welfare may be greater under a WTO-plus by some 50 percent, assuming that the reduction in NTBs applies not only to U.S. imports but to all goods and services.

The United States also has positive incentives to pursue a WTO-plus agreement with Egypt. For U.S. exporters, the "opportunity cost" of not doing so is some $1.7 billion. Although this is not a particularly large amount in relation to total U.S. exports, industries such as transportation equipment, machine tools, pharmaceuticals, and textile fabrics will be confronted with a significant decline in their exports to Egypt once the EMA and Arab League agreements are implemented. The potential export gains that can be expected from a WTO-plus are substantial and may be sufficient to induce these industries to support an Egypt-U.S. FTA. Quite apart from the foreign policy considerations, there would appear to be a mutual economic incentive for the United States and Egypt to negotiate a "deep" FTA.[40]

Arab countries should not be concerned with such a development as it does not have major implications for exports to Egypt. However, the rest of the world (nonpreferential trading partners) is likely to be adversely affected by the implementation of the FTAs. The share of total imports originating in the rest of the world declines significantly under the FTA scenarios. This is costly to Egypt as well. The government should therefore continue to pursue liberalization of its external trade barriers in conjunction with the implementation of the various FTAs. If the EMA and Arab League agreements are fully implemented and access to these markets is assured, Egypt stands to benefit most from a strategy of complementing a WTO-plus agreement with a process of unilateral liberalization.

Notes

An earlier version of this chapter was presented in September 1997 at a Brookings Institution workshop sponsored by Harvard University's Institute for Social and Economic Policy in the Middle East, and at a conference organized by the Egyptian Center for Economic Studies in Cairo in November 1997. We are grateful to Nancy Benjamin, Ahmed Galal, Wafik Grais, Robert Lawrence, Hans Löfgren, Arvind Panagariya, Will Martin, Maurice Schiff, and Arvind Subramanian for helpful comments and suggestions; to Sandy Yeats and Francis Ng for data; and to Lili Tabada for secretarial assistance. The views expressed are entirely those of the authors and should not be attributed to the World Bank.

1. This agreement was ratified by the Egyptian parliament in late 1997.

2. Viner (1950).

3. Such FTAs have already been concluded between the European Union and Israel, Jordan, Morocco, the Palestinian Authority, and Tunisia. Discussions are in progress with Egypt, Algeria, and Lebanon. See Galal and Hoekman (1997) for the Egyptian case; and Rutherford, Rutstrom, and Tarr (1993, 1995) for assessments of the Tunisian and Moroccan agreements.

4. See, for example, Galal and Hoekman (1997a).

5. Turkey is included in the EU grouping because Turkey has recently concluded an agreement to form a customs union with the European Union, which implies that any FTA with the European Union will automatically be extended to Turkey.

6. Total imports from the United States in 1996 were $3.1 billion, of which $400 million comprised exports of arms and ammunition. The latter are excluded from the simulation analyses that follow.

7. In earlier work (Konan and Maskus 1997a; Maskus and Konan 1997) it is assumed that services trade is closely complementary to merchandise trade in terms of its sources so that regional shares of services trade equal each region's share in total imports or exports of merchandise. In this chapter this assumption is only maintained for export shares of the Suez canal.

8. See Kheir-el-Din and El-Sayyed (1997); Hoekman and Djankov (1997b). However, if the fact that services are heavily protected is taken into account, average effective rates of protection for manufacturing are much smaller. See Hoekman and Djankov (1997a); and Galal and Tohamy (1997). Note, too, that total tariff revenue collections are less than what should be collected if all tariffs were fully applied owing to a variety of exemptions, including Arab League preferences, as well as circumvention. Exemptions and circumvention come at a cost, however.

9. See Hoekman and Subramanian (1997). The following discussion draws in part on that study, as well as the contributions in Galal and Hoekman (1997b).

10. Consignments that were rejected in 1993 included nuts and bolts, spare parts for cars, transformers, pressure cookers, filters, brakeshoes, ceramic tiles, light bulbs, ballpoint pens, washing machines, wheat, fresh fruit, dried fruit, sesame, frozen meat, and frozen fish. Estimates of the economic impact of the testing system do not exist. However, anecdotal evidence suggests the effect can be significant (World Bank, 1995). In 1993, for example, hundreds of tons of fro-

zen beef were rejected on the grounds that the relevant Egyptian standard (number 1522 of 1991) was violated. It has been claimed that this standard is excessively strict. It stipulates that frozen beef must have a fat content of 7 percent or less for retail sale, and once defrosted, it must have a drip content of no more than 1 percent by weight.

11. The variance in valuation and applied rates can be significant. Data provided by importers in 1995 suggest that assessed values for capital equipment may exceed invoice values by 25 percent or more, while applied tariffs may exceed the applicable statutory rates by an even wider margin. See World Bank (1995).

12. *Financial Times*, September 25, 1997, p. 8.

13. The following paragraph draws on World Bank (1998).

14. For a fuller description of the model, see Maskus and Konan (1997).

15. As discussed later in the chapter, little information is available regarding the preference margins that actually apply.

16. This assumption may seem inconsistent with the small open economy notion that Egypt is a price-taker on world markets. However, this approach is quite standard in the literature, and there is no obvious way to address this issue given the data at hand. De Melo and Robinson (1989) show that models that allow product differentiation are well behaved under a small open economy assumption; in effect the economy is a price-taker at the level of aggregate trade flows, and each region's aggregation is sufficiently distinctive to support the Armington assumption.

17. Rent seeking could well be significant in Egypt, imposing additional efficiency losses in the economy. In the absence of information about this possibility, it is ignored in order to be conservative about welfare gains from reducing NTBs. Elimination of NTBs could improve income distribution if recipients of rents are concentrated in higher income classes than those who pay them. This complication is also ignored.

18. International Monetary Fund (1994).

19. The numerous sectoral deviations from the average GST rate and exemptions and evasion of this tax are taken into account by calibrating tax rates to measures of government revenue from indirect taxes in the benchmark year. The corporate tax, or tax on operating surplus, is held constant in the analyses.

20. Taxes paid by firms on their purchases of intermediate inputs are recoverable through a tax credit, except for purchases of investment goods and some service inputs. Given insufficient information on these tax credits, it is assumed that the tax is a levy on purchases of final goods, with taxes on all inputs credited back to purchasing firms.

21. No distinction is made between domestic capital and capital inflows from foreign direct investment (FDI). The impact of trade liberalization on the volume of FDI is generally ambiguous. Tariff reduction will lower the incentive of foreign firms to service Egyptian markets with "tariff-jumping" FDI. In contrast, lower tariffs on intermediate imports may encourage export-oriented FDI. These issues are beyond the scope of the present analysis. For an exploration of the issues in the context of the EU-Tunisia agreement, see Brown, Deardorff and Stern (1997).

22. A rise in the "real exchange rate" is consistent with a depreciation of home currency, in that the price of foreign exchange per unit rises.

23. Because there is also little empirical evidence on Egyptian elasticities, labor-capital substitution is allowed to vary across industries; here, we use estimates from Harrison and others (1993). Labor-capital substitution is set at a conservative 0.50 (see table 4-2). Benchmark trade elasticities are drawn from Rutherford and others (1993). The various trade elasticities are 2.0 for substitution between domestic and imported goods, 5.0 for substitution among regional imports and for transformation between domestic output and exports, and 8.0 for transformation among regional export destinations. These parameters are consistent with the ranges of elasticities reported in Löfgren (1994). Results of sensitivity analysis with respect to the various trade elasticities are reported in Maskus and Konan (1997).

24. For a detailed discussion of the updating procedure, which involved recalibrating the model on the basis of the 1994 policy parameters, see Maskus and Konan (1997).

25. The fact that the model is based on Egypt's trade in 1990 is not much of a problem if attention is restricted to changes in welfare and trade shares, as Egypt's structure of production and trade is unlikely to have changed much since 1990. Note also that the benchmark trade shares in the model were updated to 1994.

26. Comprehensive estimates of the cost-raising effects of regulatory regimes that restrict competition in service markets are lacking. However, many case studies of individual sectors suggest that excess costs are more than 15 percent. For a discussion, see World Bank (1996) and the contributions in Galal and Hoekman (1997b).

27. Throughout the counterfactual simulations, the beverage tariff is not changed to reflect Egypt's social policy of maintaining rigorous barriers on imported alcoholic beverages. Similarly, tariffs on tobacco products are held fixed in order to reflect the fact that governments in the region will continue to impose high excises on these products for revenue and health purposes.

28. This differs from the more optimistic assumption of an 8 percent export price gain in the EU's agriculture and textile sectors used in Konan and Maskus (1997a).

29. Data for tariffs in Jordan and Lebanon were compiled from Hoekman and Djankov (1997); tariffs for Morocco and Tunisia were obtained from Rutherford and others (1993, 1995). A concordance consistent with the Egyptian IO table was developed to map tariffs into the thirty-eight sectors of the model. Tariffs were weighted by 1996 import shares, using the UN COMTRADE database.

30. This is a strong assumption, for in practice it can be expected that some cost reductions will only benefit trade with FTA partners. In the absence of information on the distribution of such benefits, we simply assume they apply across the board.

31. In this chapter we focus only on variables that are most relevant to the issue at hand: the incentives for concluding an FTA with the United States. The model is capable of generating results on a number of other variables of interest, including factor returns. These are not reported here to conserve space. In all

simulations, real returns to all factors increase, in response to enhanced efficiency in the economy.

32. Welfare changes are calculated as the percentage change in GDP, measured as Hicksian equivalent variation.

33. All nominal values reported are in 1996 U.S. dollars. Because the base data set is for 1990 (although, as mentioned, variables were updated to 1994), 1996 figures are obtained by appropriately scaling the 1990 data to reflect the increase in aggregate trade volumes between 1990 and 1996.

34. Preferences are homothetic; therefore this measure is a monotonic transformation of the Hicksian equivalent variation (see Konan and Maskus, 1997c).

35. Because the tariff tax structure in Egypt is distortionary, in principle tariff reforms that move the structure of tariffs toward greater neutrality can have a large impact in terms of raising revenue. For example, if Egypt were to adopt a 10 percent uniform tariff, the GST could be lowered by 30 percent while maintaining fiscal neutrality. Similarly, substantial efficiency and revenue collection gains can be achieved through reform of domestic tax structures. For an in-depth discussion of the impact on government revenues of piecemeal tariff reform in the Egyptian context, see Konan and Maskus (1997b).

36. With the single country model used here it is not possible to determine the welfare impact of these various FTAs on the United States. In view of the small size of the Egyptian economy, however, this will be negligible even if it is negative. What is more to the point is to explore the extent to which particular U.S. industries will find it in their interest to lobby in favor of an FTA with Egypt because they will otherwise suffer a loss in exports.

37. Havrylyshyn (1997).

38. As mentioned earlier, the Euro-Med agreement has the potential to stimulate deeper integration, but few steps have been taken in the draft agreement in this direction.

39. In the absence of detailed data on the impact of the current investment regime or policies such as government procurement practices, no attempt is made to calculate the effect of policy changes that might be induced in a WTO-plus framework.

40. On foreign policy considerations, see chapters 2 and 3 in this volume.

References

Bajo-Rubio, Oscar, and Simon Sosvilla-Rivero. 1994. "An Econometric Analysis of Foreign Direct Investment in Spain." *Southern Economic Journal* 61 (July): 104–20.

Baldwin, Richard. 1994. *Towards an Integrated Europe.* London: Centre for Economic Policy Research.

Barro, Robert J. 1991. "Economic Growth in a Cross Section of Countries." *Quarterly Journal of Economics* 106: 407–44.

Benham, Lee. 1997. "On Improving Egypt's Economic Performance: The Costs of Exchange." Working Paper 13. Cairo: Egyptian Center for Economic Studies.

Bhagwati, Jagdish. 1993. "Beyond NAFTA: Clinton's Trading Choices." *Foreign Policy* (Summer): 155–62.

Brown, Druscilla, Alan Deardorff, and Robert Stern. 1997. "Some Economic Effects of the Free Trade Agreement between Tunisia and the European Union." In *Regional Partners in Global Markets: Limits and Possibilities of the Euro-Med Agreements,* edited by Ahmed Galal and Bernard Hoekman. London: Centre for Economic Policy Research.

Burnside, Craig, and David Dollar. 1997. "Aid Policies and Growth." Policy Research Working Paper 1777. Washington, D.C.: World Bank.

De Melo, Jaime, and Sherman Robinson. 1989. "Product Differentiation and the Treatment of Foreign Trade in Computable General Equilibrium Models of Small Economies." *Journal of International Economics* 27: 47–67.

Egypt, Ministry of Economy and International Cooperation. 1996. "Egypt: Economic Profile." http://163.121.10.47/profile/economy/00.htm.

EMENA (Europe, Middle East, and North Africa) Technical Department. 1992. "Attracting Private Investment: Capitalists (Perceptions of the Investment Climate in Europe, the Middle East and North Africa)." Washington, D.C.: World Bank.

Fergany, Nader. 1994. "Egypt 2012: Education and Employment." *Almishkat,* Cairo (December).

Foreign Trade Information System. Synopsis of the Proposed North American Free Trade Agreement. http://www.sice.oas.org/root/summary/RES_TLCE.stm.

Francois, Joseph F. 1997. "External Bindings and the Credibility of Reform." In *Regional Partners in Global Markets: Limits and Possibilities of the Euro-Med Agreements*, edited by Ahmed Galal and Bernard Hoekman. Cairo: Egyptian Center for Economic Studies.

Francois, Joseph F., and W. Martin. 1995. "Multilateral Trade Rules and the Expected Cost of Protection." Discussion Paper 1214, Centre for Economic Policy Research, London (July).

Galal, Ahmed. 1996. "Which Institutions Constrain Economic Growth Most?" Working Paper 001. Cairo: Egyptian Center for Economic Studies.

Galal, Ahmed, and Bernard Hoekman. 1997a. "Egypt and the Partnership Agreement with the EU: The Road to Maximum Benefits." In *Regional Partners in Global Markets*, edited by Galal and Hoekman. Cairo: Egyptian Center for Economic Studies.

————, eds. 1997b. *Regional Partners in Global Markets: Limits and Possibilities of the Euro-Med Agreements*. Cairo: Egyptian Center for Economic Studies.

Galal, Ahmed, Leroy Jones, Pankaj Tandon, and Ingo Vogelsang. 1994. *Welfare Consequences of Selling Public Enterprises: An Empirical Analysis*. Oxford University Press.

General Agreement on Tariffs and Trade. 1994. *The Results of the Uruguay Round of Multilateral Trade Negotiations: Market Access for Goods and Services; Overview of the Results*. Geneva: General Agreement on Tariff and Trade Secretariat.

Goldberg, Moshe, Seev Hirsch, and D. M. Sassoon. 1988. "An Analysis of the American-Israeli Free Trade Agreement." *World Economy* 11(2): 281–300.

Greenaway, David, and Chris Milner. 1994. *Trade and Industrial Policy in Developing Countries: A Manual of Policy Analysis*. University of Michigan.

Haddad, Mona, and Ann Harrison. 1993. "Are There Positive Spillovers from Direct Foreign Investment? Evidence from Panel Data for Morocco." *Journal of Development Economics* 42 (October): 51–74.

Harrison, G. W., R. Jones, L. Kimbell Jr., and R. Wigle. 1993. "How Robust Is Applied General Equilibrium Modeling?" *Journal of Policy Modeling* 15: 99–115.

Havrylyshyn, Oleh. 1997. *A Global Integration Strategy for the Mediterranean Countries: Open Trade and Market Reforms*. Washington, D.C.: International Monetary Fund.

Hoekman, Bernard. 1995. "Catching up with Eastern Europe? The European Union's Mediterranean Free Trade Initiative." Policy Research Working Paper 1562. Washington, D.C.: World Bank (January).

Hoekman, Bernard, and Simeon Djankov. 1997a. "Effective Protection and Investment Incentives in Egypt and Jordan: Implications of Free Trade with Europe." *World Development* 25: 281–91.

————. 1997b. "Toward a Free Trade Agreement with the European Union: Issues and Policy Options for Egypt." In *Regional Partners in Global Markets*, edited by Galal and Hoekman. Cairo: Egyptian Center for Economic Studies.

Hoekman, Bernard, and Arvind Subramanian. 1997. "Egypt and the Uruguay Round Agreements on 'New' Issues: Laying the Groundwork for the Future." In Hana'a Keir-El-Din, ed., *Implications of the Uruguay Round on the Arab Countries*. Cairo: Dar Al-Mostaqbal Al Arabi.

IBCA (International Bank Credit Agency). 1997. "Sovereign Report: Egypt." London.

International Monetary Fund. 1994. *Government Finance Statistics Yearbook*. Washington, D.C.

Israel Ministry of Foreign Affairs. Agreement on the Establishment of a Free Trade Area between the Government of Israel and the Government of the United States of America. http://www.israel-mfa.gov.il/mfa.

Kehoe, T. 1996. "Capital Flows and North American Economic Integration." In Joseph F. Francois and Richard Baldwin, eds., *Dynamic Issues in Applied Commercial Policy Analysis*. Cambridge University Press (forthcoming).

Kheir-el-Din, Hana'a, and Hoda El-Sayed. 1997. "Potential Impact of a FTA with the EU on Egypt's Textile Industry." In Ahmed Galal and Bernard Hoekman, eds., *Regional Partners in Global Markets*. London: Centre for Economic Policy Research.

Konan, Denise, and Keith Maskus. 1997a. "A Computable General Equilibrium Analysis of Egyptian Trade Liberalization Scenarios." In Ahmed Galal and Bernard Hoekman, eds., *Regional Partners in Global Markets*. London: Centre for Economic Policy Research.

———. 1997b. "Joint Trade Liberalization and Tax Reform in a Small Open Economy: The Case of Egypt." Manuscript, University of Colorado.

———. 1997c. "Is Small Beautiful? Trade Shares and Trade Creation with Differentiated Products." Manuscript, University of Hawaii.

Krueger, Anne O. 1997. "Trade Policies for Rapid Development." Distinguished Lecture Series 9. Cairo: Egyptian Center for Economic Studies.

Lawrence, Robert Z. 1996. *Single World, Divided Nations: The Impact of International Trade on OECD Labor Markets*. Brookings.

———. 1997. "Preferential Trading Arrangements: The Traditional and the New." In Ahmed Galal and Bernard Hoekman, eds., *Regional Partners in Global Markets: Limits and Possibilities of the Euro-Med Agreements*. Cairo: Egyptian Center for Economic Studies.

Löfgren, Hans. 1994. "A Brief Survey of Elasticities for CGE Models." Paper presented to the Ford Foundation, Cairo, December 31.

Lucas, Robert E. B. 1993. "On the Determinants of Direct Foreign Investment: Evidence from East and Southern Asia." *World Development* 21 (March): 391–406.

Maskus, Keith E., and Denise Eby Konan. 1997. "Trade Liberalization in Egypt." *Review of Development Economics* 1: 275–73.

Noll, Roger G. 1997. "International Dimensions of Regulatory Reform with Applications to Egypt." Distinguished Lecture Series 8. Cairo: Egyptian Center for Economic Studies.

Page, John, and John Underwood. 1996. "Growth, the Maghreb and the European Union: Assessing the Impact of the Free Trade Agreement on Tunisia and Morocco." In Ahmed Galal and Bernard Hoekman, eds., *Regional Partners in Global Markets*. Cairo: Egyptian Center for Economic Research.

Pelzman, Joseph. 1989. "Sweetheart Deal." *International Economy*, March/April, pp. 53–56.

Radwan, Samir. 1998. "Towards Full Employment: Egypt into the 21st Century." Distinguished Lecture Series 10. Cairo: Egyptian Center for Economic Studies.

Rosen, Howard. 1989. "The U.S.-Israel Free Trade Agreement." In *More Free Trade Areas?* edited by Jeffery Schott. Washington D.C.: Institute for International Economics.

Rutherford, Thomas F., E. E. Rustrom, and David Tarr. 1993. "Morocco's Free Trade Agreement with the European Community: A Quantitative Assessment." Policy Research Working Paper 1173. Washington, D.C.: World Bank (September).

———. 1995. "The Free Trade Agreement between Tunisia and the European Union," photocopy. World Bank, Washington, D.C.

Sachs, Jeffrey. 1996. "Achieving Rapid Growth: The Road Ahead for Egypt." Distinguished Lecture Series 3. Cairo: Egyptian Center for Economic Studies.

Sachs, Jeffrey, and Andrew Warner. 1995. "Economic Reform and the Process of Global Integration." In *Brookings Papers on Economic Activity*, vol. 1, edited by William C. Brainard and George L. Perry. Brookings.

Subramanian, Arvind. 1997. "The Egyptian Stabilization Experience: An Analytical Retrospective." Working Paper 168. Cairo: Egyptian Center for Economic Studies.

Subramanian, Arvind, and Mostafa Abd-El-Latif. 1997. "The Egypt-European Union Partnership Agreement and the Egyptian Pharmaceutical Sector." In Ahmed Galal and Bernard Hoekman, eds., *Regional Partners in Global Markets*. Cairo: Egyptian Center for Economic Research.

U.S. Department of State. 1995. Country Reports on Economic Policy and Trade Practices: Mexico. http://www.state.gov/www/issues/economic/trade_reports/latin_america95/mexico.html.

U.S. Embassy. 1997. "Foreign Economic Trends and Their Implications for the United States: Arab Republic of Egypt." Cairo (July).

U.S. Trade Representative. 1996. *Annual Report of the President of the United States on the Trade Agreements Program*.

United Nations Center on Transnational Corporations (UNCTC). 1992. *The Determinants of Foreign Direct Investment: A Survey of the Evidence*. New York: United Nations.

Viner, Jacob. 1950. *The Customs Union Issue*. New York: Carnegie Endowment for International Peace.

Walker, Edward S. Jr. 1997. "United States-Egyptian Relations: Strengthening Our Partnership." *SAIS Review* (Winter–Spring): 147–62.

World Bank. 1998. "Private Sector Development in Egypt: The Status and the Challenge." World Bank Resident Mission, Cairo.

————. 1995. "Egypt: Into the Next Century." Vol. 1: "Macroeconomic Framework." Manuscript. Washington, D.C.

————. 1997. "Regionalism and Development," photocopy. Development Research Group. Washington, D.C.

Yeats, Alexander. 1996. "Export Prospects of Middle Eastern Countries." Policy Research Working Paper 1571. Washington, D.C.: World Bank.

Contributors

Ahmed Galal
World Bank

Robert Z. Lawrence
Harvard University

Bernard Hoekman
*World Bank and Centre for
  Economic Policy Research*

Keith Maskus
University of Colorado

Denise Konan
University of Hawaii

Sahar Tohamy
*Egyptian Center for
  Economic Studies*

Index

The Egyptian Center for Economic Studies

World Trade Center
1191 Corniche El Nil, 14th Floor
Cairo 11221, Egypt
Tel: (20 2) 578 1202/3/4
Fax: (20 2) 578 1205
Email: eces@eces.org.eg
Homepage: www.eces.org.eg

The Egyptian Center for Economic Studies (ECES) is an independent, non-profit research institute. It was founded in 1992 by members of Egypt's private sector. Its objective is to promote economic development in Egypt by assisting policymakers and the business community in the process of identifying and implementing reform.

ECES is keen to bring international experience to bear on Egypt's problems. By conducting and disseminating applied research and analysis of relevant issues, ECES is working to deepen understanding of the problems facing Egypt and to find appropriate solutions. Through its publications, lectures, conferences, and roundtable discussions, ECES strives to increase awareness and generate discussion of economic policy. The views and findings expressed here are those of the author(s) and should not be attributed to ECES or its board of directors.

John F. Kennedy School of Government

Harvard University
79 John F. Kennedy Street
Cambridge, MA 02134, U.S.A.
Tel: (617) 495-1100
Homepage: www.ksg.harvard.edu

The John F. Kennedy School of Government is the graduate professional school at Harvard University that serves society's demand for excellence in public service through research, teaching, and executive training. Founded in 1936 as the Harvard Graduate School of Public Administration, the school was renamed the John F. Kennedy School of Government in 1966. It has since expanded to become an international center for scholarship on effective public problem solving and leadership.

Dedicated to educating people for leadership positions in government and other forms of public service, the school is engaged in three core activities: teaching graduate students; conducting advanced programs for executives in federal, state, and local governments as well as nonprofit organizations; and undertaking major problem-solving research in public policy. The issues and problems addressed by the Kennedy School are as diverse as homelessness, urban economic development, national security, international trade, and the global environment. Contributions made by social scientists, natural scientists, government officials, business leaders, lawyers, and journalists, among others, create an environment in which research, education, and interaction are present in many forms, and where the sustaining goal is to find increasingly effective ways to serve the public interest and the central purposes of democratic societies.